Managing Ocean Resources

Other Titles in This Series

Westview Special Studies in
Natural Resources and Energy Management

Managing Ocean Resources: A Primer
edited by Robert L. Friedheim

This comprehensive collection of data and theory provides
an essential resource base for intelligent ocean-management
decisions. The book begins with essays on ocean science and
technology, social and political organization theory relating
to the oceans, and some of the problems of extracting energy
from the oceans and monitoring oceans from space. These help
the reader evaluate the management problems discussed later
in the book: those of placing economic value on the ocean;
conserving the ocean environment and marine mammals; assessing
the results of the ongoing UN Law of the Sea Conference; judg-
ing the consequences of the revolution in marine transportation
systems; determining how to assess our management policies;
and then organizing our efforts to best manage the oceans.

Robert L. Friedheim is professor of international relations and associate director for marine policy studies, Institute for Marine and Coastal Studies, University of Southern
California.

*Published in cooperation with the
Institute for Marine and Coastal Studies
University of Southern California
Los Angeles, California*

Managing Ocean Resources:
A Primer
edited by Robert L. Friedheim

Westview Press / Boulder, Colorado

Westview Special Studies in
Natural Resources and Energy Management

Published in 1979 in the United States of America by
     Westview Press, Inc.
     5500 Central Avenue
     Boulder, Colorado 80301
     Frederick A. Praeger, Publisher

Library of Congress Catalog Card Number: 79-53772
ISBN: 0-89158-572-9

Composition for this book was provided by the author.
Printed and bound in the United States of America.

Contents

Foreword

Among the many changes in our late twentieth-century world of change is the enclosure of ocean space. We are rapidly altering the rules by which we manage human affairs on the oceans. At the same time we are vastly increasing human dependence upon the oceans as a source of food, energy, and scarce minerals; as a highway for the transportation of the world's goods; as the hiding place for much of our strategic deterrent; as the border near which much of our population resides; as the focus of much of our recreational activity; and as the ultimate sink for our pollution.

With increased use comes congestion and demands for new rights concerning the use of these scarce resources. Frequently new rights-holders demand that existing rights-holders' rights be reduced or eliminated. Conflict ensues. Many of the new demands are made only because of the contemporary knowledge explosion and the rapid transformation of technology. Demands for management or regulation follow so that we do not too rapidly deplete nonrenewable resources or inadvertently destroy renewable resources.

Change concerning our "last frontier on earth" is confusing even to the well-informed citizen. Not only does the pace of change create stress, but understanding and analyzing the problems requires a background of great variety of rather abstruse subjects--physical, chemical, and biological oceanography; ecology; resource economics; and world politics. It requires a sensitivity not merely to the immediate patterns of change and their consequences, but to the longer-run patterns of change and their consequences, an intellectually much more demanding task. It also requires a reasonable grounding in the fundamental facts of the natural world. New knowledge can create new opportunities for exploration and therefore government decisions to support development or to regulate it. Knowledge of the natural world can also demonstrate to citizens demanding government action on the oceans that there are constraints upon the range of alternatives available to decision makers.

Finally, a person concerned with the future of the oceans must become aware that the oceans are a natural common. No matter how national jurisdiction has expanded, it is impossible to make the waters themselves completely compliant with human-made law. The waters will flow as nature intends, the fish move according to natural laws, the pollutants will move with the winds, tides, and currents. What this adds up to is the fact that the oceans have and will continue to have an international element. The interested citizen will quickly learn that nations' decisions concerning the ocean have a transnational impact. Reciprocity of decision will be a major concern.

The far-reaching effects of the enclosure movement on the world as we know it and the possible effects of new scientific knowledge and new engineering techniques for exploiting the ocean have been debated by specialists extensively since the middle 1960's. Too little of this technical literature has percolated down to interested laymen, students, and specialists in one aspect of the oceans who are willing to admit ignorance in other aspects of ocean affairs. This is the purpose of this book. We have assembled authors who are working at the frontiers of knowledge in the various specialities that deal with the oceans but who have the interest and ability to communicate with the aware layman--the ultimate decision makers.

We begin this collective effort to provide a well-rounded view of the oceans, its attributes, and the problems of managing its uses with two essays. Chapter 1, by Don Walsh and Donald Keach, provides a brief but very comprehensive summary of the major facts concerning the physics, chemistry, and biology of the ocean. The authors also describe the major engineering systems that are now being employed to exploit the ocean and its resources. Chapter 2, by Robert Friedheim, attempts to review the basic laws applied by humans to govern their conduct upon the oceans, to show how and why they are changing, and what basic changes in our conceptual framework is needed to explain the trend of current oceanic events. Part I, then, describes "The Nature of Ocean Space."

Part II of our citizen's guide to the oceans concentrates upon the technological opportunities and problems in our recent, and probable future, uses of ocean space. Bernard Pipkin in Chapter 3 provides a case study of the relationship of basic geology of the continental borderlands to the extraction of natural resources. Oil and gas are by definition nonrenewable resources. But the oceans can also provide energy resources that are renewable from winds, tides, currents, and thermal gradient differences. In Chapter 4, Bernard Le Mehaute analyzes some of the engineering and policy problems of these "exotic" sources of energy. Finally, Robert Hummer shows how oceanography from space is possible and what benefits there will be to mankind when the next generation of space vehicles becomes operational.

The emphasis shifts in Part III to the legal, political, and economic aspects of the use of ocean space. In Chapter 6, Ross Eckert provides a discussion of the basic tools necessary to analyze how we establish value for ocean resources. Some of humankind's activities on the oceans degrade or "insult" the ecosystem. The general nature of the problems arising from our attempt to protect the oceanic environment are addressed by Ruthann Corwin in Chapter 7. One of the problems most in need of management is the exploitation of marine mammals--principally whales and dolphins. Charles Woodhouse in Chapter 8 shows what might be done.

In 1967, then-Ambassador Arvid Pardo, in a dramatic speech to the United Nations General Assembly, brought the policy problems associated with exploitation of the ocean to the attention of the people of the world. His speech led to the establishment of the Third United Nations Law of the Sea Conference, where most of the nations of the world are trying to write a comprehensive new set of laws to allocate ocean resources and manage their uses. In Chapter 9, now Professor Arvid Pardo, often referred to as the "Father of the Law of the Sea Conference," explains why he is disappointed by the basic direction his offspring has taken. In the following chapter, Robert Friedheim analyzes Pardo's intellectual heritage and why it is important to develop a new conceptual framework for the management of ocean space. Two other problems that result from the exploitation of the ocean round out Part III. David Glickman points out significant economic, political, and managerial problems resulting from the revolution in the technology of marine transportation and port development. Ports are perforce part of the coastal zone. One of the phenomena of our time is the congestion of the coastal zone with its heavy population, pollution, and demands for amenities such as recreation. In recent years we have tried to manage the coastal zone as a separate political entity. As yet the jury is out on how effective our management efforts have been. Francis Hoole in Chapter 12 demonstrates a methodology for helping us answer questions concerning effectiveness.

In Part IV we deal briefly with larger questions of effectiveness of governmental decision makings for ocean affairs. Since the mid-1960's there has been considerable debate in the United States over whether we are organized to make effective ocean policy decisions. In the final chapter Don Walsh discusses this problem and makes a proposal for a new departure in organizing the U.S. Government to better manage its ocean affairs.

These essays evolved from a conference sponsored by the Institute for Marine and Coastal Studies (IMCS) of the University of Southern California at the Santa Barbara Museum of Natural History, November 10-11, 1977. Many people contributed to the success of the conference. We would like to acknowledge the gracious assistance of Dr. Dennis M. Power, Director of the Santa Barbara Museum of Natural History. Congressman Robert J. Lagomarsino took time from his busy schedule to address our group on ocean problems as seen from Capitol Hill. We could not have proceeded without the efforts of our hosts, moderators and citizen critics. Among them were: Mr. Gary L. Rafferty, Mr. Ted Davis, Mr. Glen Gooder, Mrs. Robert V. McLaughlin, Mr. and Mrs. Raymond K. Meyerson, Mrs. Louis L. Lancaster, Mr. Neil Robinson, Colonel H. Ben Walsh, and Mrs. Robert S. Ogilvie. Much of the brunt of the organizational work fell on the shoulders of Jim McCloud and Jon Engstrom, Director of Program Development for IMCS. Lawrence Leopold, Director of the Sea Grant Advisory Service, USC, provided his expert knowledge of coastal zone planning. Robin Friedheim and Nan Fritz contributed their professional editorial skills. I am also grateful to Toni Parker for her efforts in typing this book.

Robert Friedheim
April 1979

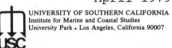

UNIVERSITY OF SOUTHERN CALIFORNIA
Institute for Marine and Coastal Studies
University Park • Los Angeles, California 90007

Managing Ocean Resources

Part I
The Nature of Ocean Space

1

Science and Engineering in the Ocean

Don Walsh and Donald L. Keach

Introduction

Of all the planets in our solar system the one we live on is distinguished by two facts: people live on it, and 71 percent of our planet is covered by water. The Pacific Ocean alone covers 34 percent of our planet or more than all of the land masses put together. Yet man's misunderstanding of ocean space is such that he gave it the name, "Earth."

It was not until the astronauts were able to get into space with their cameras that we began to understand the concept of "The Big Blue Marble," as the children's television program is so aptly named.

Figure 1.1 shows the earth from several in space, photographed by unmanned satellite over the equator in the Pacific Ocean. The center of the picture is the equator. On the right is the north-western coast of South America, Colombia, Peru, and Ecuador. Further south is the barren coast of

---

Don Walsh is Director of the Institute for Marine and Coastal Studies at the University of Southern California. He specializes in ocean policy, law of the sea, and sea power. He is co-holder of the record for the deepest manned dive to 35,800 feet in the Marianas Trench.

Donald L. Keach is Deputy Director of the Institute for Marine and Coastal Studies at the University of Southern California and Director of the USC Sea Grant Program. He specializes in ocean engineering and deep ocean research. Formerly he was Deputy Director of Navy Laboratories and Officer in Charge of Bathyscaph <u>Trieste</u>.

FIGURE 1.1
Earth Photographed from SEASAT Satellite

Source: National Aeronautics and Space Administration

Chile. To the right of the center is Central America, the Isthmus of Panama, and Mexico. Baja California is top center.

This planet is approximately 4 billion years old. Water was formed about 3.5 billion years ago, but the oceans' age, determined from dating the sediments beneath the ocean floor, is only about 250-300 million years old.

Science of the Ocean

The average depth of the world ocean is a little over two miles, about 12,000 feet. The deepest place is in the western Pacific Ocean, the Challenger Deep, where the U.S. Navy sent the Bathyscaph <u>Trieste</u> in 1960 35,800 feet, about seven miles (Figure 1.2). However, less than 2 percent of the seafloor is deeper than 20,000 feet.

The total volume of the world ocean is 360 million cubic miles. To give it some meaning or scale, <u>one</u> cubic mile of seawater would hold all of the world's population, about two billion people today.

The fluid solution that fills the ocean's volume is water with a little salt. The average salinity (saltiness) of the ocean is about 3.5 percent. In other words, there are 3.5 pounds of salt for every 100 pounds of water.

The chemical oceanographer, who studies the chemical solution we call seawater, is concerned with the ocean's chemical composition and the interaction of seawater with living organisms as well as its affect on seafloor materials.

In this cubic mile of seawater is a large volume of different basic substances, for example: 2 million tons of potassium, 4 million tons of sulphur, 6 million tons of magnesium, and enough gold to enrich many coffers. Some of these materials are extracted from sea water commercially.

The "bucket" that holds the world ocean is the world of marine geology and geophysics. Throughout the ocean floors of the world there are great systems of mid-ocean ridges and earth valleys, which essentially mark cracks dividing the earth's surface into six major crustal plates. At the boundaries of these plates the cracks are marked by deep trenches or in other places by subsea mountain ranges which have rift valleys running down their center. The world's longest mountain range (and

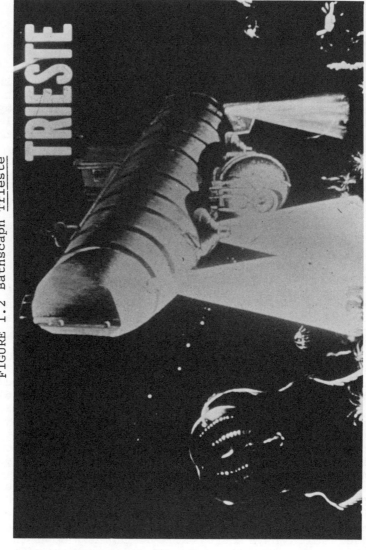

FIGURE 1.2 Bathscaph Trieste

Source: U.S. Navy

4

rift valley) is the Atlantic Ocean's Mid-Atlantic Ridge. This mountain range is nearly 10,000 miles long as it curves around the tip of Africa into the Indian Ocean. Some of the mountain peaks which stick up above the sea surface are known to us as the Canaries, Madeira, Azores Islands.

Iceland sits right on the rift valley, where the seafloor is being formed. Crustal material is forced up from the earth's interior, then gradually spreads to the east and west. Along the crack of the rift valley is extensive volcanic activity. Iceland's very active terrain is a surface manifestation of this usually unseen seafloor activity. Occasionally it is seen, as when the entire Island of Surtsey pushed up out of the ocean floor near Iceland before the fascinated gaze of scientists and laymen. Iceland's hot thermal springs and frequent volcanic eruptions help remind its people that they live on a crack in the earth.

The fact that the ocean floor is so young partially explains why it is continually being formed and destroyed. As the seafloor creeps out toward the continents it moves underneath the continental crustal masses. The continents are much lighter (less dense) than the ocean floor. They "float" on top of the denser ocean floor crust. The ocean floor crust at this point is "recycled" back into the interior of the earth and will appear millions of millions of years later back at the rift valley where it is again pushed out to form new seafloor.

This theory was debated for many years. It could not be proved until we developed a drill ship that could be used for geological research. In the rift valley the rocks and sediments should be very young because they would be newly formed. Moving away from the rift either east or west these materials would get progressively older. This would prove that it is the place of seafloor formation.

The <u>Glomar Challenger</u> a very sophisticated ship operated by the Global Marine Corporation for the National Science Foundation, was able to do this sort of drilling throughout the world along these coastal plate boundaries. They were able to determine the evolution and movement of the plates over the past ten years, and the theories have been proved correct.

The most important part of the ocean floor to us is the continental shelf. From the shoreline to a water depth of about 600 feet at its outer edge, the continental shelf represents only about 8.5 percent of total seafloor area. But there all offshore

gas and oil is located, most of man's fisheries
activities are conducted, and most of the pollution
damage takes place.

The "continental slope" is the transition slope
from the continental shelf to the continental rise,
and then finally to the deep ocean floor at an average water depth of about two miles. Here is the
province of the physical oceanographer, the scientist who studies currents, waves, and tides,--"the
motions of the oceans." How do the great currents
in the world ocean circulate?

Figure 1.3 is a drawing of the major surface
currents. Along the U.S. Atlantic coast is the Gulf
Stream, the largest and best-known current in the
world. It comes up through the Florida straits and
along the east coast of the United States before
moving away from the coast and across the North
Atlantic ocean.

The darker shading is the warmer climate; the
white is the coldest water. The Gulf Stream carries
the warm tropical water across the North Atlantic
to Europe. England and Scotland, far to the north,
are kept relatively warm by those bands of warm
water from the Gulf Stream.

The surface circulation (currents) of the world
ocean are technically called "wind-driven circulation." In the northern hemisphere, the general cir-
culatin is clockwise; in the southern hemisphere,
counterclockwise. The patterns are quite symmet-
rical.

How does the system work? The planet's principal energy source, the sun, heats up the ocean.
The warm ocean water re-radiates part of this heat
back into the atmosphere. In addition, the sun
boils off (evaporates) some water from the ocean
surface so both heat and moisture are put into the
atmosphere, forming clouds and large convective
cells of heated air. In the same way the atmosphere is being heated from the bottom by the solar
energy that has been absorbed by the seawater.
Water has great storage capacity for heat energy.

The sun stores up the heat in the ocean rather
quickly, the ocean re-radiates that heat rather
slowly, and vertical circulation of air above the
ocean begins. As heated air rises from the sea surface it is replaced by cooler air drawn in along
the sea surface. The friction of the air rubbing
along the sea surface creates surface waves and
currents.

Some of the water that is carred into the atmosphere goes over land, forms clouds, and falls

FIGURE 1.3 Major Ocean Surface Current

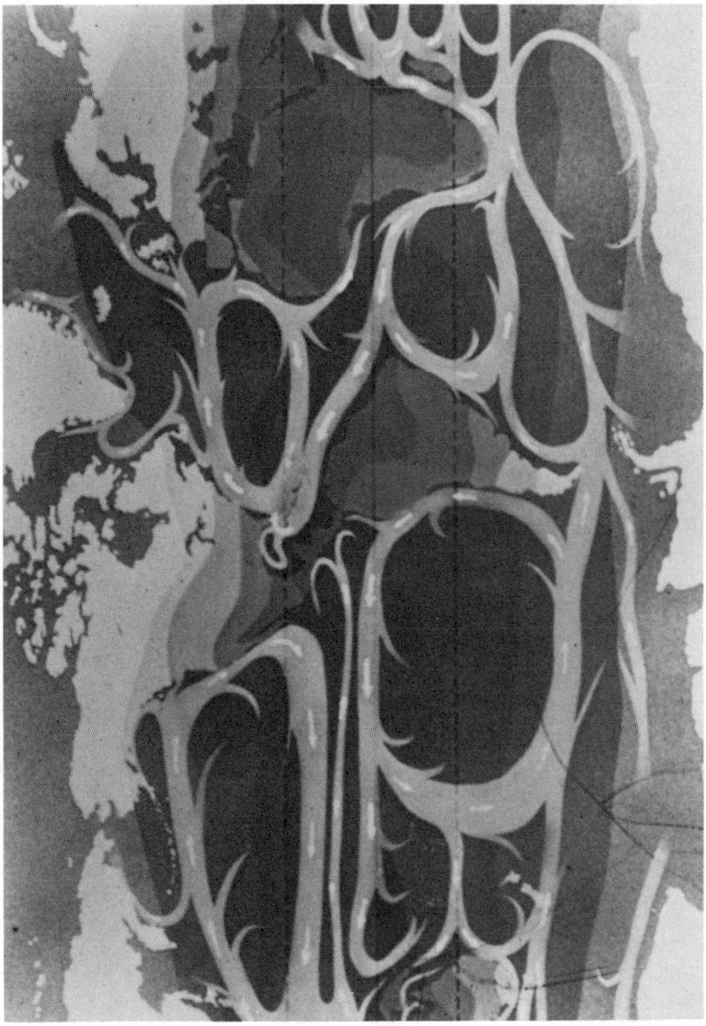

Source: U.S. Navy

7

out as fresh water. Most of it eventually returns to the sea in a continuous cycle. We call this process "the hydrologic cycle." Water used on land for man's needs also carries pollutants, nutrients, and other substances from the land back into the sea.

The importance of "the great river in the sky" is demonstrated by the fact that nearly two-thirds of all the rain, or precipitable water, that falls east of the Rockies in the United States comes from the Gulf of Mexico. This atmospheric flow of warm, moist air crosses the Gulf Coast of the southern United States, flows into the central plains states, and then falls out as water when atmospheric weather conditions are right to form rain.

The giant vertical circulations of this "boiling atmosphere" heated from below by the oceans, combined with the rotation of our planet, creates planetary winds. These permanent winds flow in fixed directional patterns across the ocean's surface. In many regions the wind blows from one direction all year round with a very steady velocity, for example, the "trade winds." As that wind pushes on the water surface, it moves and the surface circulation patterns, "the wind-driven circulation," begin.

As noted earlier, the global surface circulation also acts as a giant global thermostat. The tropics have excess heat and excess energy. There needs to be some natural mechanism to keep this region from heating up. We know its density from weather records that go back hundreds of years. The earth's temperature fluctuates very little over long periods of time.

The circulation of the ocean and atmosphere act as a natural mechanism (a kind of global-basic hot water central heating system). The boiler is in the tropics, the surface current circulations are piping, carrying heat up into parts of the planet where there is a heat deficit, such as the polar and subpolar regions. Heat is slowly released whenever the circulation enters a cooler region. The great wind-driven circulation is also a way of distributing, primarily through the circulating water, the earth's heat throughout the planet to keep the planet's climate in balance.

While the oceans' surface waters are important to man, there are other, more complex deep current circulations in the oceans. These are the "density" currents.

8

Seawater in the oceans has varying degrees of buoyancy which are influenced by its temperature and salinity. More cold and more salt make heavier water. Cold, salty water is very heavy, and when it flows out into the ocean it tends to sink to the bottom. These flows are density currents--deep, very slow-moving currents propelled by gravity as the heavy waters try to flow "downhill." The principal source of deep-density currents is the Antarctic, where very cold salty water is formed in the Weddell Sea. It sinks to the bottom and moves along the floor of the Atlantic and Pacific, flowing slowly north with remarkable extent. Remnants of "Antarctic Water" can be found at the bottom of the Gulf of Mexico. Another major source is in the straits between Labrador and Greenland.

A specialized case is the very warm Mediterranean Sea. As the sun evaporates the fresh water from its surface, not cold, but very salty water, is left. The heavy saline water sinks to the bottom of the Mediterranean, flows along the sea floor and out over the sill at Gilbraltar. Fresh Atlantic water flows in at the top, which in turn is "boiled off," becomes heavy and flows back out at the bottom. This is a good example of a deep, as opposed to wind-driven, circulation.

There is another important circulation, more localized, called "upwelling." It is found in certain coastal areas where the winds blow parallel to shore. Generally the coastal wind blows the surface layer away. Water from beneath comes up to replace the water that has been blown off at the top. The deep water is full of nutrients such as heavy dissolved minerals and organic matter. They gradually sink to the bottom, where there are few animals to consume them. When circulated, this "deep water" and its contents become the ocean's food supply. "Recycling" through this vertical circulation provides surface waters that are extremely rich in nutrients, capable of supporting a high degree of biological activity.

Upwelling areas are not found everywhere in the world, but in places are very prominent, such as off the west coast of South America. Peru often ranks as one of the largest fishing nations in the world by catch tonnage, not because they have a high technology fishing industry but because of the hugh catch of anchovy within a few miles of the Peruvian coast.

The life cycle in the sea begins with sunlight, which stimulates the growth of microscopic plankton

9

plants called phytoplankton--"grass of the sea." The next larger plankton are called "zooplankton"-- microscopic animals which feed on that "grass." Thus the "food chain" begins. Fish such as the her- ring, anchovy, and smelt feed directly on the plank- ton; they are in turn eaten by other fish, and so on. Figure 1.4 is a graphic example of the food chain.

This figure shows what it takes to put one pound of weight on a person. It takes 10,000 pounds of phytoplankton, the microscopic plants, to make a half ton of zooplankton. And it takes a half ton of zooplankton to make 100 pounds of anchovy. The anchovy in turn will make ten pounds of tuna which finally makes one pound of person. In other words, there is a ten-to-one reduction at each stage of the food chain.

Let us now consider where people prefer to live and relate that to those areas of the oceans that are usually the areas of greatest value and human activity. Historically pooulation clusters have concentrated near lakes, river valleys, and coast- lines. There are many reasons for this, including ease of transportation, availability of food from the waters, recreational opportunities, and usually better weather than foud inland.

Ocean areas of greatest interest tend to be on and near the continental shelf areas of the ocean world. Until we begin to exploit the minerals of the deep ocean or find "exotic" biological biolog- ical resources there, man has comparatively few in- terests in the open oceans. They are, for example, not that productive for fisheries. The waters over the continental shelves are generally more produc- tive in biological resources and the land beneath for oil and gas. Because these areas are near the coast and therefore accessible to large populations, we also find a high level of pollution. One of our most serious problems is the competition for use of the same areas on and over the continental shelf for fishing, producing oil and gas, shipping, recre- ation, and dumping grounds.

Studying the Sea

Man's interest, formal and informal, in the oceans goes back centuries. In about 4 B.C. Aristotle did some good work as a marine biologist in examing and recording various marine species that he found near his home in the Mediterranean.

10

FIGURE 1.4 Marine Food Chain

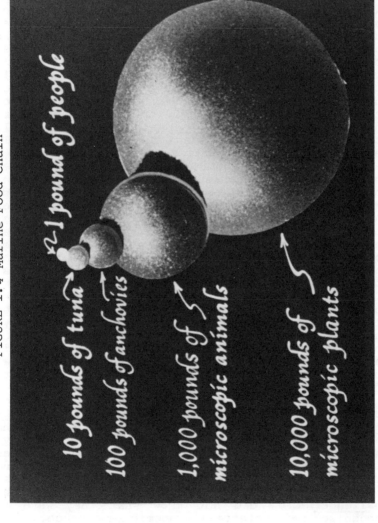

Source: U.S. Navy

More recently, only 200 years ago, an organized study of the sea took on a great importance during the time that Benjamin Franklin was Postmaster General of the United States. He noticed that certain of the mail vessels sailing between the United States and England consistently made much better time than others, regularly cutting several days off their voyages. He discovered that some mariners had known about the phenomenon of the Gulf Stream. He began to take the information that the ship captains would bring in on what courses they navigated as well as the temperatures and colors of the water they sailed through. He knew the Gulf Stream was both much warmer and lighter colored than the water on either side. By charting this information, all our mail ships going to Europe could get in the Gulf Stream and enjoy the extra push of the current. On the return trip they could navigate to stay out of it so they would not be held up. This resulted in one of the earliest navigational charts of the Gulf Stream and helped to make U.S. shipping of mail, people, and goods more efficient.

In the 1840's a U.S. Navy lieutenant, Matthew Fontaine Maury, extended this work by cataloging worldwide ship's log observations made by whaling captains and merchant mariners. He put it together in chart form and sent it back to them so that they could have more effective navigation, faster passages, and avoiding ocean hazards. As they became convinced of the value of these charts, more and more captains joined in reporting hazards, rocks, and shoals that had never been seen on a map before.

Maury himself launched several expeditions at sea, measuring depths and making rudimentary studies of ocean flora and fauna. Unfortunately, Maury, who had begun the U.S. Navy's hydrographic office in 1840, joined the Confederate Navy in the Civil War. Afterwards he never regained his prominence, and ended his professional years at the University of Virginia teaching meteorology.

The first scientific voyage in the history of oceanography was from 1872 to 1876. The H.M.S Challenger, a British Navy frigate leased to the Royal Society, undertook round-the-world study voyage. "The Challenger Expedition Reports," more than fifty volumes, resulted from this expedition and are still being used. The first known manganese nodules were picked up on this voyage, although the Challenger crew did not know what they were or recognize their potential economic importance.

The biggest stimulation for the advancement of marine sciences has come in times of war. During both World War I and World War II the major navies needed to know more about the oceans to operate effectively and to counter enemy submarines. In fact, up until ten years ago the U.S. Navy was the largest single supporter of oceanography in the United States.

Today oceanographers use a wide variety of very sophisticated research platforms which are complex floating laboratories. Modern research ships have hundreds of different measuring devices, sensors, and samplers.

There are also exotic, specialized ships such as the Glomar Challenger. As noted earlier, this vessel is used for drilling into the earth's crust in the deep oceans, sampling ocean sediments and rock structures far beneath the sea floor in water as deep as 16,000 feet, three miles down. In one case, the men were working north of Hawaii when a storm came up. They moved off the site, pulled up the drill string, and returned to Hawaii. They marked the seafloor hole with an acoustic beeper. After the storm, they returned and put the drill string down in the same hole. That might be compared to standing on top of the Empire State Building with a friend on the sidewalk and lowering a thread down throught the eye of a needle in his hand. This is the state of ocean technology and scientific sophistication possible in marine research today.

Other specialized craft are equally capable, for example, the Navy's See Sea a simple fifty-foot catamaran. Ten feet beneath it is a small observation chamber with two large four-foot-diameter plastic bubble windows, accommodating two scientists who study the behavior of sharks, seaweed beds, etc. Their work on the feeding behavior of sharks has been important in learning how to protect swimmers.

Many submersibles have been used over the last twenty years to take scientists into the sea. Submersibles are particularly useful because they take the trained mind and eyes into the environment. For the parts of oceanography that are observational sciences, this is very important. In marine biology or marine geology the scientist wants to observe a rock, bottom sediments, or animals of various sorts directly. In shallower depths, to about 150 feet, many marine scientists use SCUBA diving equipment.

Underwater vehicles are powerful tools for to-day's oceanographer. The submersible <u>Alvin</u> located at the Woods Hole Oceanographic Institution, has been used extensively to explore the rift valley in the Mid-Atlantic Ridge. Scientists have been able to observe on site the place where the lava has come out of the interior of the earth and the new sea floor is being formed.

For places where fairly simple, long-term measurements are needed, a large, moored buoy can be used. For example, the Navy developed the "Monster Buoy," forty feet in diameter. Some of these units are anchored in the North Pacific Ocean in two to three miles' depth of water, remaining year-round and sending daily messages by radio or via satellite. They take many kinds of meteorological and oceanographic measurements and are cheaper to buy and operate than research ships.

For certain kinds of measurement in shallower, nearshore waters where mobility is not required, oceanographic towers can be set up as fixed platforms. One well-known tower is the Navy's oceanographic tower, located about two miles off Mission Beach near San Diego, California.

On the edge of the atmosphere and in space, oceanographers use aircraft and spacecraft, when one needs to be able to put the ocean at arm's length. This is especially true in the observation and measurement of large-scale phenomena, for example, to capture the entire Gulf Stream in a single photograph.

Uses of the Ocean

The earliest organized use of the sea was probably fishing, going back thousands of years to the time when people from a coastal village would get together, build a boat, and cooperate in fishing rather than acting as individual hunters. It follows from this that naval architecture is the oldest form of ocean engineering. Ports and coastal engineering were next; when the boat came home, there had to be a place to store it safely.

Generally speaking, the ocean in early times was used as a highway of commerce, exploration, and conquest. Only since this century began has man really begun to consider the ocean as having an intrinsic value as well as having an exploitable third dimension of depth.

Presently the most prominent resource extraction activity in the world ocean is offshore gas and oil. About 25 percent of all gas and oil in the world is provided from beneath the ocean. By 1980 it is estimated that about one-third of the gas and oil in the world will come from beneath the sea. Most of this, of course, is on the continental shelf. The world oil industry is producing off the coasts of 85 different nations throughout the world, and they have done exploratory drilling off the coasts of about 110 nations throughout the world.

Also on the seafloor are found the manganese nodule deposits. Manganese nodules are a complex form of manganese, copper, cobalt, and nickel. It's of ore quality, usually high grade. The formation of these is through a process we don't completely understand right now. The nodules, which look like dirt clods or lumps, can vary from peanut sized to those weighing many pounds, 30 to 40 pounds in some cases.

Nodules are found in all the major ocean basins and have enormous economic potential (Figure 1.5). In the Pacific most of them seem to be arrayed along the tropical latitudes. These are those that will be first "mined." Generally the best quality nodules are found in water depths of about 16,000 feet. They are most valuable right now for their nickel, but the copper, cobalt, and manganese are also very valuable byproducts.

Conventional dredging has always been quite important in coastal and port engineering. But dredges also have been developed to work the placer gravel deposits off rivers, such as the Yukon River in Alaska where gold has been carried down the river and deposited in the offshore delta area.

Off southwest Africa a few years ago the same idea was applied to dredging for diamonds. The rivers running through the areas which had diamond deposits would pick up some of these diamonds and carry them out to sea. Dredging for the diamonds was successful.

The most widely used dredging application is probably land reclamation. The most famous example of course is Holland, which has added one-third of the total area of their nation through judicious dredging activities over the past few hundred years.

Seawater may become another major energy source. A very small percentage, about 2 percent, of all of the water in the world is fresh water. About 80 percent of the fresh water in the world is

FIGURE 1.5 Ferromanganese Deposits in the Pacific Ocean

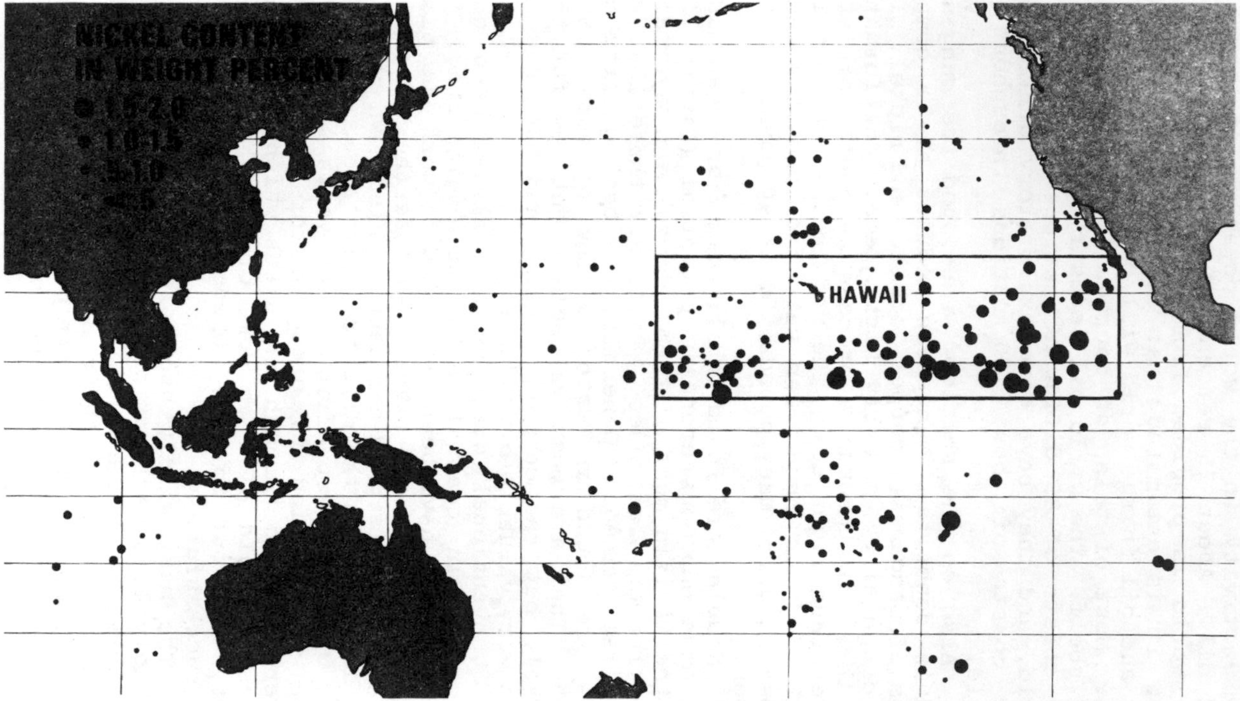

Source: Ocean Minerals Company

16

tied up in the great ice formations in the Arctic, Greenland, Iceland, and the Antarctic. At the South Pole, for example, the ice cap is over 11,000 feet thick. If all of the earth's ice mass were to melt, New York City would be covered by water.

As mentioned earlier, the sun has a role in storing heat energy in the sea. But the tidal motions resulting from the gravitational forces exercised on the earth by the moon and by the sun can be harnessed. The moon moves in its prescribed path and the earth moves slightly in response to these forces. More important, the water film on the earth responds considerably more since oceans are a free fluid. These movements are called tides. In some places there are two tides a day, in others one, in some places no tide at all. Tidal ranges as high as fifty feet are found in a few areas, which can be used as a source of hydroelectric power. Tidal power plants now exist in France and the People's Republic of China. In the United States the potential exists in Alaska. In Nova Scotia, Canada, the Bay of Fundy offers good possibilities.

Today freshwater is produced from over 600 desalinization plants throughtout the world which have a total capacity of over 2 billion gallons a day. Generally speaking, the desalinization of water is done in areas where energy is relatively cheap, such as the Middle East, or where the demand for water and lack of alternative supply makes it acceptable to use expensive fuels to create power used in the extraction process. It is an expensive way to produce water, but where there is little choice it is done. For example, the city of Key West, located at the end of the Florida Keys, gets most of its water from desalinization.

Seawater is also a source of minerals. About 50 percent of the magnesium and about 80 percent of the bromine produced in the United States is provided through the processing of seawater.

World trade uses the ocean as a highway of commerce. There are about 130 coastal states in the world. Most of them are developing nations, and, therefore, they primarily export raw materials and import finished products.

World trade routes for petroleum, materials and goods continue to increase in frequency. However, even today, 98 percent of all goods that move in the world go by ship at some point between manufacturer and consumer. Also over 50 percent of all our petroleum is imported into the United States by tankers. So we cannot slight the importance of maritime commerce and trade throughout the world.

The United States is really an island-state, very dependent upon the sea. Approximately 87 percent of all raw materials needed to maintain industry and life are transported over the ocean.

Today the world catch in fisheries is about 66 million tons. It was 70 million tons four years ago. However, only about 6 percent of the world's catch is taken out of the Indian Ocean. This indicates tht there may be still room for some growth in that ocean. This may provide essential food in the near future. The "world hunger belt" consists of the regions where the majority of the poeple of the world lives. This belt roughly consists of the tropics and subtropics, where the poeple suffer from malnutrition, especially protein malnutrition.

Marine plants also are quite useful. The giant California kelp is one of the fastest growing plants in the world. It grows up to three feet a day under ideal conditions. These plants are used widely for industrial purposes and foods. Recently both plants and animals have being subjected to very careful examination as a source of pharmaceuticals. There are some excellent, large scientific medical programs looking at living marine organisms as sources of drugs from the sea.

The farming of the ocean, "aquaculture," is beginning to take on greater importance. Ten percent of the world's fish harvest today is accomplished through man-induced cultivation. In the United States it is not a very large enterprise, but its is growing rapidly. Forty percent of our oysters, about 80 percent of our catfish, and 100 percent of our trout are farmed, even though some of this production may be put into fee fishing lakes. We rarely remember when we had to pay five dollars to catch a trout in a fee fishing lake that it was likely that the trout began life in somebody's pond or farm under controlled farming conditions.

Marine recreation is an area that many of us also do not think about when we consider uses of the sea. But today total annual spending in marine recreation in the United States is 8.5 billion dollars. By anybody's index that is a big industry. Not surprisingly, the fishing catch of sports fishermen in the United States far exceeds the catch of our commercial fisheries.

We can even build houses beneath the sea for people to live in. It is technically possible. It is still not known if it is desirable or cost effective, but technology exists to do work of this sort. Perhaps someday as our coastal zone become more crowded, we will find undersea living residences in the shallow waters of coastal zones where some sunlight can still penetrate through the ocean's depths.

Presently there is some serious work being done on the floating city concept. At the Okinawa Ocean Exposition a few years ago, the Japanese actually had a full scale city block module of a floating city installed offshore. The Japanese are thinking of putting in floating city components in Tokyo Bay to expand the limits of the cities of Tokyo and Yokohama. These are on the surface, however, not "cities under the sea."

Useful Work in the Sea — Ocean Engineering

Today there is an ever increasing demand to apply human ingenuity to solving human problems by making more effective use of the sea. Floating cities are only one of many exciting potential applications. Applying human ingenuity to solve these types of problems is the task of the ocean engineer. Ocean engineering is simply the application of science and technology to do useful work in the oceans. Ocean engineering integrates an understanding of the physical, biological, geological, and chemical properties of the oceans into the engineering process, with appropriate accommodations to political, economic, and social factors as well.

Ocean engineers must have a thorough grounding in fundamental ocean science. The ocean is a difficult environment in which to do useful work. To work successfully in the oceans requires understanding of a number of contraints imposed by nature upon those who wish to exploit the bounty of the ocean. The engineer must consider the enormous forces posed by waves, currents, and pressure. He must also consider the problem of accurate navigation and positioning of ships and platforms on and within the vast ocean areas. While the temperature range within the oceans is small, temperatures in the polar regions can present serious engineering problems as a result of surface ice and seafloor permafrost zones. Salinity is a major challenge to the engineer because of its highly corrosive properties. Marine life too is an important consideration in that some forms create major fouling problems

19

for ships and structures while others can destroy pilings and other structures exposed to the environment. The noise created by some species of marine life can seriously disrupt systems which rely on sound transmission within the oceans. The nature of the bottom is important in designing bottom mounted structures, pipelines, and cable placement.

The ocean engineer must also have a good working knowledge of the legal, political, and economic costs of the work he wishes to do at sea. It is not enough merely to recognize that a proposed project is technically feasible. An ocean engineer's work is also subject to economic pressures, and the current and waves emanating from the political system. The ocean engineer must understand these constraints and must also contribute to the answer to questions such as:

-Does it solve a human need;

-Is the project cost-effective;

-Can it be done within the existing legal guidelines; and,

-Can the project's product operate efficiently and still pollute excessively?

Working in the Sea

We have looked briefly at some of the sea's characteristics which are of concern to the engineer and at some of the uses which are the basis for working in the sea. Now let us take a look at ocean engineering advances being made in the process of developing these uses of the sea.

In marine transportation, traditional ship designs are being augmented by higher speed types including catamarans, air cushion vehicles (Figure 1.6) which literally ride on a cushion of air, and hydrofoils which ride on foils, keeping the hull clear of the water. Conventional ship hulls designs are also being supplanted by special purpose carriers such as liquid natural gas, roll-on-roll-off, and container ships. Massive oil tankers of 500,000 tons and larger are being constructed.

In the fishing industry, ocean engineering advances have been relatively minor. Eighty percent of all conventional species are still caught with round nets as they were hundreds of years ago. Twentieth-century technology, in fact, is respon-

FIGURE 1.6 U.S. Navy Air Cushion Vehicle

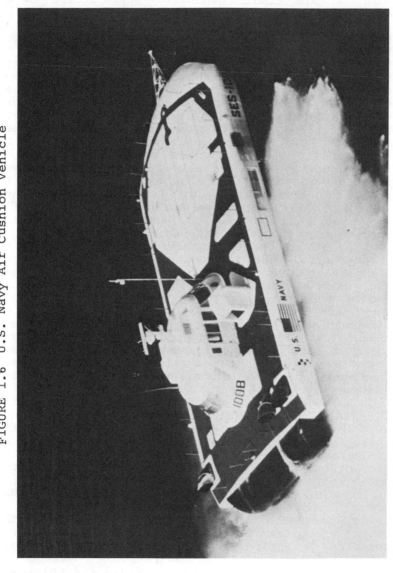

Source: U.S. Navy

21

sible for not more than 1 percent of the fish harvest. The ocean engineering advances which have been made over the past forty years are improvements in equipment such as introducing nylon line for nets, improved navigation, better echo sounders and more capable fishing vessels. Aquaculture is an area where rapid improvements might be made in the future. While at present less than 10 percent of the worlds' fish and shellfish catch are harvested through this means, intense study is underway to develop better feeds, reduce disease, and increase the survival rate of the young. Many of the ocean engineering gains made in the past century have been driven by national defense needs. Submarine warfare, antisubmarine warfare, and strategic deterrence requirements have been the driving force behind a vast array of technological advances which have benefited every segment of society. Much of the technology which results in a fleet of nuclear powered ballistic missile submarines enables us to probe the ocean depths for resources with manned and unmanned submersibles and divers, develop offshore oil and gas fields, and extract manganese nodules from the deep seafloor.

With the impetus derived from an expanding technological base, world population explosion, and diminishing land resources, civil uses of the sea and related ocean engineering activities have burgeoned over the past forty years. Foremost among these are those associated with the extraction of offshore oil and gas. Geophysical prospecting, exploratory drilling, and production activities are going on simultaneously around the world in increasingly deeper water. Fixed oil production platforms, once limited to very shallow seas, are now being emplaced in water depths of 1,000 feet. Drilling rigs have been built which are capable of operating in water depths of 12,000 feet and well heads and oil distribution systems have been designed for operation on the seafloor, nearly independent of the surface.

Oil and gas are not the only energy-related ocean engineering taking place. Under the direction of the U.S. Department of Energy a 100 megawatt (MW) Ocean Thermal Energy Conversion (OTEC) system is being designed. This system takes advantage of the stored energy represented by large temperature differences in tropical oceans between surface and deep water. The principle of operation is similar to that in a steam power-plant. A fluid (in this case ammonia) is exposed to warm surface water where it evaporates with the vapor passing through a turbine which generates electricity. The vapor is then passed through a heat exchanger which circulates cold water brought up from the deep ocean. The vapor then returns to the liquid state and the cycle starts over. The ocean engineering challenge in this system is represented by the fact that the pipe bringing the cold water to the surface is some 120 feet in diameter and 3,000 feet long. The other potential ocean energy sources mentioned earlier have been exploited to a limited extent, but the energy density and conversion efficiency is so low that it is difficult to harness these sources economically.

The engineering associated with dredging and marine mining has changed little over the years except in the area of deep ocean mining. Manganese nodules, which exist throughout the world's oceans in water depths of 12,000-16,000 feet, have been the focus of a recent major ocean engineering effort. Two basic seagoing dredge designs have been developed. One involves a continous line of buckets attached to a cable. The buckets scoop up the potato-shaped nodules from the seafloor, bring them to the surface where they are dumped into a barge and the empty buckets lowered again to the seafloor. The second design vacuums the nodules up in a continuous flow of water moving through a pipe to the surface. They will then be dewatered, dried off, and transferred to bulk carrier ships to bring them to port for processing. (See Figure 1.7).

There are significant ocean engineering advances being made in conjunction with other uses of the sea. Deep water ports and artificial islands are being designed for installation in many places throughout the world. Enormous subsea oil storage and transfer facilities are being installed adjacent to major oil fields. Recovery systems for salvage of vessels and other large objects lying in deep water have been constructed. In support of scientific research, a deep sea drilling system is under design which can take samples of the earth's crust 35,000 feet below the surface of the ocean. These are just a few of the many major engineering activities taking place throughout the world today.

There is one potential use of the sea which periodically captures the public imagination and which poses interesting ocean engineering problems. It is the possibility of solving part of the world's fresh water distribution problem by moving icebergs from the Polar seas to arid regions of the earth.

23

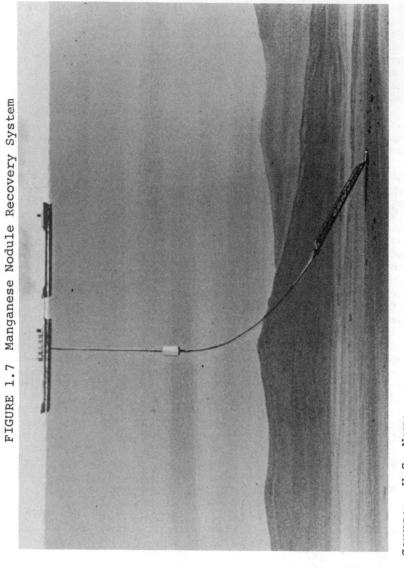

FIGURE 1.7 Manganese Nodule Recovery System

Source: U.S. Navy

24

The engineering required to move a melting ice mass, weighing billions of tons, with a draft of nearly a fifth of a mile, through thousands of miles of ocean is a significant problem indeed. Perhaps the most interesting thing about it, as with virtually any other use of the sea we might think of, is that it is not a question of might it be done with today's technology, but rather is it feasible considering the political, social, and economic climate of the world in which we live?

Conclusion

Today there are "doom prophets" who are sure the oceans are dying. They are either neo-Malthusians or persons to whom ecology is an ideology rather than a field of science. We do not subscribe to such a belief. We do not believe that the end is at hand. However, it is true that we can do serious damage to the ocean if we are not concerned about its use. This is especially true in the more vulnerable coastal areas over the continental shelf.

We should remember that, "the ocean's bottom is more interesting than the moon's behind." Four times more is spent by the United States for space programs than for ocean programs. That is, the budget for the National Aeronautics and Space Administration is 4 billion dollars a year while the national ocean research budget is only about 1 billion dollars a year. We are not advocating the lowering of the space budget. Rather we do advocate equity with respect to studying the principal planetary feature that comprises 71 percent of our spacecraft called "Earth." Understanding the water planet is a priority if we are to sustain human progress.

2

The Political, Economic, and Legal Ocean

Robert L. Friedheim

The United Nations Conference on the Law of
the Sea (UNOLS) has now dragged through nine sessions of bargaining between representatives of approximately 150 states. When it began there was
hope that it would establish a "new constitution"
for the oceans. Despite the lack of a treaty the
twelve years of negotiations have profundly altered
the substance and thrust of ocean law, but usually
not in the direction the proponents of a new constitution for the oceans would have wished.[1] Indeed, the order of the day is enclosure of ocean
space by nation states. This is confirmed in what
there is of a draft treaty (Revised Single Negotiating Text) at UNCLOS or via the plethora of unilateral national declarations that are being issued
even as the official printer's ink has dried. Most
of these lay claim for the coastal state to a 200-
mile fishing conservation zone or 200-mile economic
zone. If all coastal states adopt 200-mile zones,
it is estimated that 36 percent of ocean space could
soon be enclosed.[2]

While the direction of ocean law and policy is
unmistakable, there is no widely believed "theory"
or "conceptional framework" (paradigm) of ocean enclosure that would help explain what it is all
about. Most ocean theoreticians have characterized
enclosure as a set of "second-best" solutions, or a
single politically based solution to a thoroughly

Robert Friedheim is Associate Director of the Institute for Marine and Coastal Studies and Professor
of International Relations at the University of
Southern California. He is the author of numerous
works on ocean policy.

multifaceted set of problems. The absence of a conceptual framework creates many problems, practical as well as theoretical. Only when we have a paradigm for ocean enclosure can we provide ourselves a guide to make the details of our policies consistent with each other. A new conceptual framework is especially important because of the breakdown of the present one. Thus, one of the important priorities today in ocean policies is the development of a general theory of ocean enclosure. The purpose of this chapter is to suggest some elements that might be useful in the development of a new paradigm for the management of ocean space. Since one of the most profound short-run changes relates to fisheries, this chapter will concentrate on the reasons for the creation of national fishery zones. Before discussing the new, we must explore the old. We will examine the traditional framework for governing world fishing, describe how and why it has broken down, elucidate the present historical trends, and then look at four elements that might be incorporated into a new paradigm.

The Past: Oceans an International Common

The traditional "paradigm" for managing human affairs on the oceans is based upon the notion that the oceans are an international commons and that the resources found therein are common property resources. To specialists these terms mean that beyond a narrow band of national sovereign jurisdiction (the territorial sea), no claimant may claim an exclusive right to ocean areas or ocean resources. The resources found in the common are said to belong to all (res communis) or to no one (res nullius). Until our time, the distinction between them had no operational meaning although many legal treatises were written on the subject. What is important to remember is that under this status, ocean resources can be used by anyone who is a member of the "community." Communal use implies that no government or authority has the ability to assign rights over the resources. The only limit on a member of the community who uses ocean areas or takes ocean resources is that the user not interfere with the right of other members of the community to use ocean area or resource. This does not mean that there is no law imposed upon the user of the common, but it is for the most part the national law of the user who carries his own particularistic law with him when he enters the aqua incognita of ocean

27

space. This is the law of the wandering tribe or
clan of antiquity.

Fish and other biological products of the sea
are the most widely used common-property resources
of the world ocean. There are four characteristics
possessed by fish when they are utilized communally.[4] First, they have economic value. People
wish to use them, mostly for consumption. As a result, people will put an economic value upon them.
Second, fish are indivisible. Until our times it
was impossible to "brand" ocean fish or keep them
behind fences or in herds so that it was virtually
impossible to distinguish ownership even if some
claimants tried. Because fish in commercial quantities were essentially nonterritorial (a wandering
resource, although today we know only some pelagic
fish migrate long distances, other migrate relatively short distances, and some are highly "territorial"), they are said by economists to be in
"joint supply." Third, fish can be by any unit
among competing social units. Thus, Frenchmen,
Americans, Japanese all may find the fish equally
desirable. Finally, there is no control of access
to fishing. All fishermen have the right to take
as much fish as they desire or are capable of catching. Fishing in the common sea is what might be
characterized as an open access system. While they
are in the sea, the fish belong to no one or everyone, but once they are in the hold of a fishing vessel, title to them passes to the fisherman. They
are his. All attempts to control or manage fishing
must be voluntary and by agreement between the
representatives of the fisherman. There are few
incentives to show restraint. While they have
worked on occasion, "voluntary" controls have not
provided an overall solution to the problem.

The entire system of treating fishing as a common-property resource has resulted in a situation
in which there is no market price for ocean fish.
This does not mean there is no monetary value to a
fish in the fish market, but rather the fish per se
has no cost. This is unlike the situation with
domestic animals. If we lead a lamb to slaughter
we pay for the cost of the lamb as well as the cost
of employing its slaughterer when we buy a cut of
lamb in a meat market. Fish that originated as a
common-property resource has no such cost, only the
cost of its slaughterer (the fisherman) are included
in the price of the fish in the market. Thus, it
is reasonable to claim that the private price of

28

the goods (the fish) does not reflect the full social costs.

By treating ocean resources such as fish as common property, we have created a system in which most incentives lead to waste in the catching effort and overexploitation of the available stocks. Since the stocks are "wild" and humankind has little positive direct control over the reproduction cycles of these wild creatures, the consequences would be disastrous.

Let us move from economic to legal terms. Since the early seventeenth century and until recently, the Western world, and because of Western imperialism, most of the remainder of the world has perceived the oceans as governed by the doctrine of "freedom of the seas." This has been a powerful and simple paradigmatic idea. The seas are open to the use of all. From this we derive the notion that no jurisdiction is subject to the sovereign control of any single nation-state. Indeed, only the obligation not to interfere with the rights of others limits the freedom of users of the seas. The right to transit over the open waters of the world, the right to take ocean resources on a nonexclusive basis (law of capture), and the right to be governed by one's own national laws only when using the ocean all derive from the freedom of the seas.

All of these ideas were consolidated in Hugo Grotius' famous justification of the rights of the Dutch East India Company, Mare Liberum (1698). These prescriptions for managing and regulating human affairs on the oceans have lasted for 370 years. Before we examine why they are succumbing to attack, we should understand that they lasted because they had social utility. They were attacked by writers in Grotius' own times--Seldon in Mare Clausem (1635), Seraphin de Frietas in De Justo Imperio (1625), and Welwood in De Dominio Maris (1615). European rulers and prelates before and after attempted to impose the opposite rule of closed seas or enclosure. But all ultimately failed. For 370 years the doctrine was the dominant organizing idea because it allowed individuals and nation states access to ocean areas and resources at the lowest social cost possible. It encouraged entrepreneurial behavior. While there were no significant problems of scarcity, it was clearly an appropriate guide to human uses of the oceans.

The Present: Finite Oceans

It is not remarkable that Grotius' freedom of the seas broke down. It is remarkable how long it took to break down. Grotius' idea in Mare Liberum was a paradigm not because it was a profound or noble set of ideals (although on this basis it is still easy to find defenders of Grotius), but because it was a reasonable empirical description of the state of the oceans and the relationship of man's tools for taming the oceans to its fundamental nature. The oceans are a "natural" commons as long as man's tools for control or management are primitive. The waters flow and respect no manmade boundaries. Ocean currents begin and end where nature puts them even if they flow through many areas claimed by different political jurisdictions. Fish do not obey manmade law of territoriality. Fences are difficult to construct in the oceans. As a result of this recognition of the "natural" commonness of the ocean, Grotius could make three assumptions: first, that the oceans are infinite and therefore not appropriable; second, that the ocean's resources are inexhaustible and therefore there are no problems of scarcity; and third, that the oceans are perpetually pure and therefore there is nothing human beings can do to degrade them to the point of irreversibility. As long as they were approximately true, the paradigm remained a reasonable description of reality and could survive. When these conditions began to break down, the paradigm began to be attacked.

All three assumptions are under attack today. Many analysts would argue that indeed the oceans are finite, their resources--renewable and nonrenewable--are being rapidly exhausted, and that the oceans are being heavily polluted even if they are not, at present, "dying."

The assumption that the oceans were infinite presumed they were not divisible, or at least not easily divisible. But today, we can put "fences" in the ocean. Even if they do not work perfectly, they work better than the "fences" of Spain and Portugal who were allowed to divide up the Atlantic Ocean 100 leagues west of the Azores in a Papal Bull of Alexander VI in 1493. Those fences failed because the moral authority of the Pope was in question during the Protestant Reformation, and also because Spain and Portugal's fences could not keep out of the New World the freebooting raids of Sir Francis Drake and Sir John Hawkins. To use modern

30

terminology, the costs of keeping them out ("enforcement costs") were prohibitive and if a public authority cannot keep out those it prohibits, it does not "effectively occupy" and therefore cannot treat an area as its own territory or property. Today it is more probable that political entities do have the tools to effectively occupy.

As scientists learn more about the oceans we can no longer believe that its stocks of renewable and nonrenewable resources are inexhaustible. Many more desirable stocks of fish are being overfished, according to Food and Agriculture Organization data. The total world catch of around 70 million metric tons may be expanded--some estimate to 100 million metric tons--but it is finite and to exploit further will require the use of sea creatures such as krill not currently much consumed by human beings. Nonrenewable resources are by definition exhaustible. Although we have only recently begun the exploitation of ocean oil and gas and have hardly begun the exploitation of ocean minerals (in particular manganese nodules) and therefore do not face worldwide short-run problems of absolute scarcity, we would do well to consider how profligate exploitation of land-based resources has created problems of scarcity.

Finally, we know we can degrade the oceans by man's acts, deliberate and unplanned ("externalities"). We must consider for the first time the possibility of doing irreversible damage. Attempts to clean up after the fact and muddling through until we must face the problem will not do if some of the assumptions of environmentalists prove real. But we need not go that far. Pollution usually begins by fouling one's own nest. There are significant costs involved. There are incentives to do something remedial before we create irreversible changes. But it is difficult to enforce such anti-pollution measures if our paradigm insists that significant damage cannot be done to the infinite ocean.

All of Grotius' assumptions are subject to attack because of the enormous transformations in science and technology. With new technology we can meet the tests of effective occupation ("fences" composed of fast ships, surveillance aircraft, radar, sonar, black-box electronics to identify who is entitled to be in a claimed zone, etc.), we can exploit fish to the point of exhaustion (radar, sonar, factory ships, nylon nets, power winches, preservation by freezing, and distribution systems), and we can pour pollutants into the ocean through outfalls, the air, stream runoffs, and deliberate and accidental vessel discharges.

Freedom of the seas in an age of scarcity with powerful human tools of exploitation available may be the freedom to destroy. Without some remedial action to eliminate the incentives to destroy by eliminating the commons, the world may face on the oceans the "tragedy of the Commons" described by Garrett Hardin.[5] Hardin used the movement to enclose commons pasture land in eighteenth century England as a metaphor for our present problems with renewable resources. It is a powerful lesson. Let us assume that there are ten farmers and each runs one sheep on the common. Each sheep has an adequate share of the common-property resource--grass--to eat to keep it healthy. Let us further assume that one ambitious farmer in analyzing the situation sees that if he puts another sheep on the common that he will be better off. Thus, we now have eleven sheep where there were once ten. Each of the eleven sheep now have 10 percent less to eat, a reduction in their intake that probably would not seriously affect their health and productivity.

However, some of the remaining nine farmers decide that the tenth farmer by making himself relatively better off is making them worse off. Thus, in response the second farmer puts a twelfth sheep on the commons (reducing the grass each gets by 17 percent, and the third farmer puts a thirteenth sheep on the commons (reducing the grass each gets by 24 percent). At this point the thirteen sheep are getting thinner, producing less meat, wool, and milk but surviving. When the fourth farmer puts the fourteenth sheep on the commons (reducing grass available by 29 percent), and the fifth farmer puts the fifteenth sheep (reducing stock available per sheep to 34 percent less than we started), disaster looms. Malnutrition would probably reduce productivity, raise the cost of ownership to each farmer as he tries to find alternative feed, and perhaps seriously affect the health of a substantial number of the fifteen sheep. Indeed, there might be a heavy mortality rate among the sheep, forcing many of the ten farmers to suffer losses. This would be a tragedy.

To avoid the tragedy of the commons, there are three avenues of approach that should be explored in search of a solution. We could 1) ask the farmers to negotiate to not expand their sheep to more than one per farmer or, if expansion has already

taken place, to voluntarily reduce the sheep population to what the grass can sustain; 2) teach farmers
to grow more grass so that more sheep can be sustained; or 3) enclose the existing common and divide
it up into parcels so that each farmer can manage
or mismanage a separate parcel, hopefully giving
him an incentive not to mismanage.

The first solution--voluntary agreement--while
popular as a nostrum, is very difficult to work effectively. Inherent in it is a classic problem best
illustrated by game theory, the prisoner's dilemma.
In this situation each farmer knows that if all
farmers voluntarily agree to stop at or return to
ten sheep, they will all be better off, albeit at a
relatively low-income level. Each farmer also knows
that if the other farmers show restraint but he runs
extra sheep on the common, he will be much better
off. But if all farmers hope that other shows restraint but none does so, they will all be much
worse off. If each farmer uses individual "ration-
ality" and tries to maximize his short-run gains,
the probabilities are great that the participants
individually will choose the worst collective
decision.[6]

Unfortunately, the world fishing industry may
be in the prisoner's dilemma situation. The voluntary international agreements to control or reduce
fishing have staved off the day of disaster but they
have not solved the problem. Ocean fishing still
suffers from the boom-or-bust behavior pattern.
Many specific fisheries have gone through the cycles
of good catches, overcapitalization of the fishing
effort and overutilization of labor, and then decline. While we should not eliminate bargaining
among equals as a tool of solving our problem
strictly as a result of insights from game theory
(if only because people are not perfect self-maxi-
mizers and do at times have a concern with the wel-
fare of others), the empirical evidence that world
fishing problems have not been solved by voluntary
agreement is very strong.

The second solution also looks intriguing. We
would all be better off if we could increase the
stock or resource that we share in common. If the
farmers had learned to grow more grass, they would
have been able to sustain more sheep. Under those
circumstances many of them would have been better
off. This solution is one frequently suggested
today in the light of humankind's recent scientific
and technical mastery. Indeed, growing more has
been suggested as the solution to the world's

general food problem. Fertilizers, hybrid and "miracle" grains, pesticides, etc. have substantially increased the capacity to grow food crops on land. Some analysts believe that despite these advances, it will not be possible to avoid tragedy because of the "law of increasing costs."[7] Others are more optimistic.[8] But no experienced observer believes that aquaculture (deliberate human cultivation of ocean biological resources) is sufficiently well developed as to make a significant contribution to the world's protein supply in the foreseeable future.[9] It would not nearly replace the protein from wild fish if humankind were so foolish as to act out the tragedy of the commons.

The third solution--enclosure--while unattractive on many grounds, appears to be the solution, if only by default. To avoid the tragedy, divide up the area or common among the claimants (farmers or nation states on behalf of their fishermen) so that within each subset of territory the new "owner" can manage his resource. In other words, the purpose is to take away the characteristic of commonness or availability to all that makes the resource a common-property resource. The "owner" under enclosure will have the right to control entry into the exploitation of the stock. If the owner is "rational" and concerned with the long-run protection of his asset he will not allow the asset to be overexploited merely to make a short-run gain. Rather, he should exploit it for his own benefit on a sustainable-yield basis.

Enclosure: The Only Solution

Whether enclosure is the "best" solution to the problem of the despoilation of the common or not, it may be the only feasible solution. If we judge by the haste with which states are creating 200-mile fishing or economic zones, it appears that national leaders today believe it is a solution or at least an opportunity to "get a handle" on the problem, or a hand on the resource. Of course, it just may be part of a larger prisoner's dilemma where states take the most rational individual short-run policy course available which when aggregated may lead to a common disaster.

At the least, what enclosure is likely to do is shift the burden of its costs to the weakest, or least well established, or geographically most dependent members of the system. We should not assume

34

that our ten farmers will divide the commons into ten equal shares, on which they will each run one sheep. It is more likely that the farmers with two or three sheep will insist that at least the status quo be preserved so that they will be no worse off after enclosure than before. This would mean that they would be given enough land and grass to keep their larger number of sheep and that the farmers with one sheep each would have to divide up the remainder.

Enclosure can be a rough-and-ready solution to the problem. We should remember that some farmers were allocated too little land to sustain themselves or no land at all in the real world of eighteenth-century England. Today a number of former users of the marine resources found within 200 miles of the coast of other states are increasingly finding themselves on the outside of the fence looking in. From a systemic point of view, as Hardin remarked, "injustice is preferable to total ruin."[10] But if a state, a farmer, or fisherman is among those who are ruined, that person or entity (subsystem) has little incentive to cooperate in such a solution. The method of enclosure the world seems to have chosen creates equity problems. There are indeed losers in the current rush to enclose. By comparison with their coastal neighbors who are expanding their jurisdiction and thereby increasing the chance of increasing their wealth, landlocked states are worse off. Traditional ocean users--navies, steamship companies, some fishermen--fear they may be worse off than under freedom of the seas because there will be less open ocean for them to use freely. They fear at least a rise in their costs as the complexity of coastal state regulations that they must obey increases. Their worst fear is eventual exclusion from 200-mile functional zones as they harden into 200-mile "sovereign" zones as a result of "creeping jurisdiction." States such as Japan, the USSR, and other distant-water fishing states who have a substantial investment in distant-water fleets and/or a considerable food dependence on distant-water catches are also losers, since the new national quotas they must obey (if they continue to have access) are lower than their previous catches.

What we tend to overlook today is that there is more than one type of enclosure that the world community could have attempted. A clear choice has been made only recently. It was possible to enclose in a centralized as well as decentralized manner.

35

A number of schemes of central enclosure have been offered. Inherent in most of them is the notion of ending the freedom of the seas over the oceans of the world, preserving the wholeness of the ocean system and <u>not</u> subdividing it. Ownership (defined functionally and not in sovereign terms) is transferred to the world system under the notion that the oceans are the "common heritage of mankind," allowing a new comprehensive organization for the management of ocean space acting as agent for the world community to allocate the permitted uses of ocean space so as to avoid the boom-or-bust activity characteristic of common property.

Theoretically, if adopted, this would be the optimal solution for the management of ocean resources.[11] Although there was a hope that the UN Law of the Sea Conference would take such a proposal seriously during the preliminary phases of the negotiation, as the delegates proceeded from Caracas to Geneva to New York, it became clear that the scheme fell victim to an acting out of the prisoner's dilemma in the real world.[12] The common heritage of mankind is, of course, the solution that can be arrived at only by cooperation of all of the negotiators. Alas, most delegates preferred not to give their consent and chose instead the alternative that would provide them the most short-run benefit--national or decentralized enclosure.

The trend to extend national jurisdiction outward, to subdivide the formerly open ocean into larger national subsets of the world system, is unmistakable and perhaps irreversible. Considering the existing overexploitation and rapid development of technologies that would allow humans to stage further assaults upon common resources, the only thing the world community could not do was do nothing. The system of freedom of the seas was no longer "homeostatic," or self-correcting.[13]

The ocean system may not be in equilibrium for some time, at least until the status of all the oceans is settled. 200 miles is no magic number. It represents the demands of the West-coast Latin American states in response to the Truman Proclamation of 1945 (the first modern attempt of a nation to appropriate ocean resources). The figure 200 miles was chosen because it was said to be the maximum extent of the Humboldt Current, which brings nutrients on which fish feed. We have no reason to believe that states will terminate the enclosure movement at 200 miles if valuable resources are found beyond 200 miles or if the exploitation of resources beyond 200 miles leads to typical common-property problems. The present developments may be a mere interlude in the long-run changes underway.

Where are we now in respect to ocean enclosure? Rather far along. Not only have a substantial number of coastal developing states declared for 200-mile zones but virtually all coastal states--even those who originally opposed the Latin American-inspired push to 200 miles--have either passed unilateral legislation, or have announced they soon will. This includes the United States, the USSR, Canada, the European Community, and even the state most dependent upon its distant-water rights--Japan.

The decrees vary as to wording and intent. We do not know the full extent of rights they intend to demand or obligations they will accept. But there are certain common threads found in all the different decrees. First, they have announced they can effectively occupy; how well remains to be seen. The variations in the capacity to occupy effectively is a potential source of conflict in the foreseeable future. Second, they all have announced that they intend to treat the economic zone essentially as territory; that is, within the 200-mile zone the law of the coastal state (or the subject over which they demanded jurisdiction) will rule, rather than users bringing their own law with them as they wander into the zone. All who enter the area are expected to obey. Third, all 200-mile-zone states intend to reduce, control, or manage entry into the exploitation of the resources of the zone. The degree to which they will eliminate all common-property attributes vary (some may merely create common-property problems in "their" area of the oceans), but the days of operating on the law of capture along the coastas of other states is over.

Most knowledgeable observers believe that national enclosure is a second-best solution to the problem of the misuse of common property. This is particularly true for living resources. It is impossible for human beings to order fish to stop their movement through ocean space. The right to allocate which the coastal states have assigned to themselves may be used to redistribute wealth only and not to create rational management schemes for the resources. It is a system dependent upon drawing borders, but borders in the ocean world are still hard to define, draw, and defend. The cost of drawing and defending these borders is still to be determined, thus we have no idea of the benefit to cost ratio. Finally, national enclosure does not handle the question of equity well and this may raise the costs of enclosure for both those included as well as those excluded. But the world is involved in the middle of a round of enclosures. Enclosure decrees will not work at all unless we propound a "theory" of enclosures that satisfied most interested parties so that we can get on with implementing enclosure at the lowest possible cost.

How to Enclose?

We have already narrowed the area of choice. The decision to enclose most of the coastal waters of the world seems to have been made. This makes the choices we have yet to make all the more important. How we will enclose still leaves each enclosing state with many important decisions. Making these decisions will be easier and the results would be better if we had a "paradigm" to guide us. Below are some suggested elements that should be considered in constructing such an organizing concept. In a "theory" of enclosure we must account for 1) order, 2) justice, 3) efficacy, and 4) residual commonness.

If there is any reason why national enclosure may have been necessary, it is that there was no authority structure to turn to so as to create and maintain order. As we saw earlier, the world might have created a superordinate world agency, but the probabilities were that its authority would have been suspect and its capacity limited. The most basic justification for political systems is their capacity to create order. Without authority there is no capacity to assign rights, and without authority to create order there is no capacity to effectively defend rights. A political structure such as a nation state can create order within a territory (its law will "run" within the area), and assign rights to claimants.

We must be very clear that the purpose of enclosure is to create order so that rights can be assigned and that resources can be sensibly allocated on something other than a first-come, first-served basis. If this is so, then we must distinguish between the right of the coastal state to assign right within its zone and the capacity of coastal state to monopolize for itself or its citizens all rights within the zone. Probably, those

38

states that make such a distinction and assign to themselves only the former will have their claim to authority recognized by other states. It is much more questionable whether disappointed claimants to resource use or the states that represent them will recognize the latter.

Justice is, of course, in the eye of the beholder. What is just to one claimant in a process involving interaction will be seen by another party as injustice. Unfortunately, it will not be easy to separate attempts to impose order from attempts to use monopoly powers to change wealth patterns, or to exclude "foreigners." There is a strong component of nationalism in enclosure efforts. For some states, enclosure is a counter-response to "foreigners" stealing "their" resources even though in no legal sense were the resources beyond their territorial sea or fishing contigious zone "theirs."

Nevertheless, the sense of justice of the coastal population is involved in making the enclosure decision concerning resources near their coasts. We must be aware in the enclosure process that justice is a two-way street in the reallocation of, at least, resources that are already exploited. Justice is important for its own sake. It is also important for conflict reduction. Finally, it is important in order to make enclosure work at the least cost. As enclosure takes hold, and as coastal states make an investment in managing their resources, justice questions seen as access to wild fish or unappropriated mineral or energy resources will become less important. Until then, an awareness of the harm one state can do to another state and its citizens is an essential component of a worldwide 200-mile zone theory.

Ultimately, the question historians will ask about late twentieth-century ocean enclosure is-- did it work? Was it an effective system of allocating and managing resources? Did it create a system of sustainable yields? Did it minimize economic waste? Did it distribute the benefits to the concerned parties in such a way as to create an incentive for cooperative behavior?

As we have seen, national enclosure is _not_ the optimal system of social control of formerly common-property resources. It ends open entry only in a limited area. It does not solve the problem at all for highly migratory (pelagic) stocks. It does not guarantee efficient practices in the zone. It further decentralizes or "Balkanizes" ocean space. It puts management powers into the hands of entities

(nation-states) that do not have successful historical records of guarding and promoting their existing ocean resources.

It is much too early to tell if nation-states
will use their new-found enclosure rights poorly or
reasonably well. At the present juncture we can
say only that, in the views of some specialists, it
is not likely to be the optimal system. But we must
not be lead by this to ask the wrong question. The
important question is not "is it the perfect system"
but rather, "on a net assessment does it do well
enough?" Are there more good than bad results?
Kenneth Boulding reminds us, "the best is the worst
enemy of the good."[14] Can we achieve the good by
enclosure? is the question we must answer.[15]

Finally, we cannot treat water property as if
it were land property. There will always be some
degree of residual commonness in water areas placed
under the exclusive jurisdiction of the coastal
state. This is one reason, despite the reduction
of justice questions in the future, that justice
questions will always be with us in dealing with
the area and resources of ocean space. We cannot
stop the fish from moving. We cannot expect, even
if we choose to foul only our own nest by dumping
pollutants into "our" waters, that what we do in
our waters will not affect the interests of others.
Since ocean space is multi-dimensional, we will always have multiple-use problems in offshore zones.
Fish, seabed areas under which there are the most
promising indicatiors of exploitable oil and gas,
narrow straits, the best recreation areas, the most
fragile ecological zones, and the most heavily trav-
eled sea lanes, may also substantially overlap in a
geographic sense. Each user would prefer an exclusive right. In constructing a theory of enclosure
we very seldom can grant such an exclusive right.
The waters flow.

The perceptive reader, at this point, may observe that it is all very well to take the four
elements discussed into account in trying to create
a new paradigm for enclosing ocean space, but that
an amalgamation of these four ideas leaves us with
an increadibly complex set of materials to construct
a social theory. One of the glories of the freedom
of the seas was its simplicity. A theory of a ter-
ritorially-based water area such as we have begun
to sketch but one that allows some degree of transnational penetration, is not simple, and this is
regrettable. There is a great loss in "understand-

ability." But it is an ever more complex world and we need more complex concepts to understand it.

Notes

1. Ambassador Elliott Richardson, *Press Release* USUN-57 (77), July 20, 1977.

2. "Theoretical Areal Allocations of Seabed for Coastal States . . ." *International Boundary Study, Series A, Limits in the Sea,* No. 46, August 12, 1972 (Washington D.C.: Office of the Geographer).

3. There is now an extensive literature on common-property theory as it applies to the fishery. Some highlights are: H. Scott Gordon "The Economic Theory of a Common Property Resource: The Fishery." *Journal of Political Economy,* 62 (1954), pp. 124-42; Anthony D. Scott, "The Fishery: The Objectives of Sole Ownership," *Journal of Political Economy,* 63 (1955), pp. 116-24; James A. Crutchfield and Arnold Zeller, "Economic Aspects of the Pacific Halibut Fishery," *Fishery Industrial Research* 1:1 (Washington: GPO, 1963); Francis T. Christy, Jr. and Anthony D. Scott, *The Common Wealth in Ocean Fisheries* (Baltimore: Johns Hopkins Press, 1965).

4. Francis T. Christy, Jr., "Property Rights In The World Ocean," *Natural Resources Journal* 15:4 (October 1975), p. 696.

5. Garrett Hardin, "The Tragedy of the Commons," *Science* 162 (December 13, 1968), pp. 1243-48.

6. Martin Shubik, *Game Theory and Related Approaches to Social Behavior* (New York: Wiley, 1964), p. 36 ff.

7. D.D. Meadows, D.L. Meadows, J. Randers. W.W. Behrens, III, *The Limits to Growth* (New York: Universe Books, 1972), pp. 45-54.

8. H. Kahn, W. Brown, and L. Martel, *The Next 200 Years* (New York: Morrow, 1976) pp. 106-38.

9. L. B. Brown and G. W. Finsterbusch, *Man and His Environment: Food* (New York: Harper & Row, 1972), p. 98.

10. Hardin, "Tragedy . . ." *Science,* p. 1247.

11. For a discussion of economic theory arguments see: R. L. Friedheim, "Understanding the Debate On Ocean Resources," *Monograph Series In World Affairs,* 6:3 (1968-69), pp. 21-24, for a recent restatement of the common heritage notion see: Elizabeth M. Borgese and Arvid Pardo, "Ocean Management" in *Reshaping the International Order,* Jan Tinbergen, Coordinator (New York: Dutton, 1976), pp. 305-17.

12. Aaron Danzig, 'A Funny Thing Happened to the Common Heritage on the Way to the Sea," *San Diego Law Review* 12 (1975), pp. 655-665.

13. For an application of cybernetic notions to political systems, see: John Steinbruner, *The Cybernetic Theory of Decision* (Princeton: Princeton University Press, 1974).

14. This author's notes from a lecture by Kenneth E. Boulding, "Societal Aspects of Ocean Food and Energy," Second International Marine Technology Conference, Texas A&M University, October 5-8, 1976.

15. One well-known fishery economist, James A. Crutchfield, is "moderately optimistic." "Evaluation of the Conference By An Economist," *Economic Impacts of Extended Fisheries Jurisdiction* (Ann Arbor: Ann Arbor Science, 1977), p. 382.

Part II
Technical Problems and Opportunities for Using Ocean Space

3

Southern California Continental Borderland and Extraction of Natural Resources

Bernard W. Pipkin

Many geologists involved in marine reseach are interested in edges or the continental margins, because that is where much of the world's gas and oil are found, and where most of the living natural resources occur.

Types of Continental Margins

We can categorize the continental margins where the land meets the sea into three types. The Atlantic-type margin occurs around the Atlantic Ocean, consisting of a broad flat continental shelf becoming steeper at the continental slope which leads down to the deep seafloor. Somewhere along the continental slope the true domain of the ocean basin begins and the continental rocks end. Along the coast of Chile and Peru the shelves are very narrow. There the slopes lead down into deep trenches which are the focal points of very strong earthquakes and explosive volcanic activity. This is the second or Pacific-type margin, to be found off the coast of South America, the Aleutians, and the Japanese islands. However, the west coast of the United States, and particularly the seafloor off southern California, is quite different. It consists of a series of north-northwest trending

Bernard W. Pipkin is Associate Professor of Geological Sciences at the University of Southern California. He is the author of many publications on earth sciences as well as a recent book on oceanography.

mountain ranges and valleys which are simply an off-shore continuation of the land topography.

It is so unique that in 1941, Francis Shepard and K.O. Emery named this the "continental borderland." There are nineteen basins (valleys) offshore that vary in length from twenty to eighty miles and in width from about two to twenty miles, with a total area about equal to that of the Adriatic Sea (Figure 3.1). Geologists agree that the trend of these ridges and basins is fault-controlled, that is, the basins represent portions of the earth's crust that have foundered along bordering faults, with the relatively up-faulted blocks forming the inter-basin ridges. The Santa Barbara basin is 2,000 feet deep and it rises southward to form the Santa Rosa-Santa Cruz ridge, clearly visible from land. This is a submarine bank or ridge that rose above sea level and became a series of islands.

Let us take a similar excursion southward from Los Angeles. The Los Angeles Basin represents an ancient marine basin that is now filled with sediment as much as 16,000 feet thick! During the filling of the Los Angeles Basin, Palos Verdes was a submerged bank and eventually became an island much like Catalina Island is today. As one proceeds offshore from Palos Verdes Peninsula the seafloor drops into the San Pedro Basin, which is about 3,000 feet deep, rises to Catalina Island, which is a ridge above the ocean level, and then drops again into the Catalina Basin, which is about 4,200 feet deep. Continuing on a southerly track one encounters San Clemente Island, then San Nicholas Basin, which is about 5,000 feet deep, then the Tanner Cortez Bank, and finally into an unnamed basin which is around 5,600 feet deep. From this area begins the true continental slope, known as the Patton Escarpment, that leads down into the deep sea (Figure 3.1).

On Cortez Bank is probably one of the most interesting geographical phenomena of the continental borderland. There is a shoal that is only four meters deep. Some charts show it as little as twelve feet deep at low tide. It is called Bishop Rock. Many fascinating enterprises have been proposed for Bishop Rock, such as an abalone farm and also a new community constructed on fill 110 miles offshore.

The basins get deeper offshore. The reason for this is that the near-shore basins are filling with sediment faster than the offshore ones. Closer to terrigenous sources of sediment the rate at which

46

FIGURE 3.1 Perspective of Continental Borderland Off Southern California

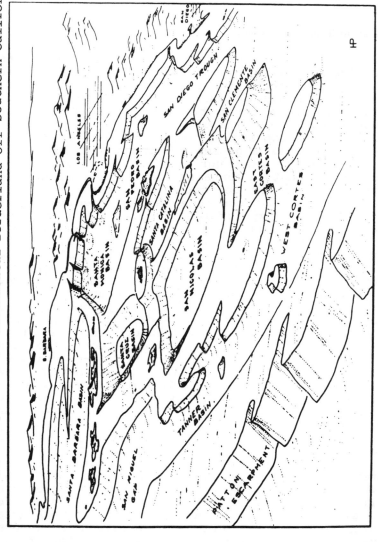

Source: John Duncan

47

these basins fill is more rapid. Some sedimentation rates were determined in the San Pedro Basin using Carbon 14, and they showed an average filling of the basins of fifty-four centimeters--about 1.7 feet --in a thousand years. A little arithmetic shows that the San Pedro Basin would fill in about 5 million years, allowing for compaction of the sediments.

History of Basins and Ridges

Now the question arises "when did the basins and ridges form and what was the continental margin like in the past?" We can get evidence for this from the geology of islands like Santa Rosa and Catalina. There is to be seen in the Santa Ynez range behind Santa Barbara a bright red sandstone that is also exposed on Santa Rosa Island. It is not unusual that a geologic formation should occur on both the mainland and an offshore island except that this sandstone contains fossils of land animals and was obviously deposited by streams on land. Therefore, we must conclude that the sediments exposed in these two different places were at one time connected and part of a continuous landmass that had a common source of sedimentary material. Similarly, a coarse-grained sedimentary rock containing a distinctive blue-green mineral known as glaucophane is found along the cliffs at Laguna Beach. It is obviously a land-laid deposit and its source must have been to the west. The only possible area that could have served as a source for this distinctive mineral is Catalina Island. Thus, at this time, Catalina and the mainland were connected with no intervening marine basin. Using well-established fossil evidence, we know that the offshore basins and ridges we call the borderland formed in Mid-Tertiary time, on the order of 10 to 20 million years ago. Since the ocean basins as they occur today are about 250 million years old, therefore, our borderland is a very young geologic feature indeed.

The northern Channel Islands are of particular interest because they represent an extension of the east-west trending Transverse Ranges of southern California. The rocks and structures found offshore are similar to those forming the Santa Inez-Santa Monica mountains onshore. It appears that at one time the islands formed a continuous mountain range and may have existed as a narrow peninsula during

48

much of Pleistocene time. Evidence for this is to be found in the fossil elephants on Santa Rosa Island. All known species of the mainland elephants were ten to fourteen feet in shoulder height, whereas the island forms are only six to nine feet high. The elephants migrated there when the Santa Monica mountains extended seaward and later, as the peninsula was faulted into a series of islands, the mammoth population evolved dwarfed forms. This was probably due to the low carrying capacity of the island forage.

Natural Resources

Marine research at the University of Southern California has been deeply involved in the study of the processes that deepen and maintain submarine canyons. There are no less than a dozen well-mapped and named canyons from Point Conception to the Mexican Border. Hueneme, Mugu, Dume, Santa Monica, and Scripps-La Jolla Canyons are just a few. The heads of many submarine canyons intervene in the transport of sediment in the nearshore area and trap sand that would normally be supplied to beaches downcurrent. We estimate that a million cubic yards per year of sand is trapped by the canyons to eventually flow downslope into the offshore basins. Inasmuch as most of our beaches are suffering from a lack of natural sand supply, this loss has a large impact on beach erosion. The value of such sand in the current market is very close to two dollars per cubic yard, thus we are looking at a resource loss of about $2 million.

Mining of hard minerals off southern California is a long way off. Phosphate nodules on nearby bank tops cannot compete with the abundant land supplies of that mineral (at least 100 years in the United States). Sand and gravel reserves have yet to be demonstrated and mining them is fraught with environmental problems. The biggest resource is oil and gas and will continue to be so for decades. The outer continental shelf (OCS) offers the greatest promise at this time. The Baltimore Canyon tract on the east coast contains at least 1.4 billion barrels of oil, and it has been estimated that OCS California contains no less than 14 billion barrels. This is greater than the Alaskan Arctic slope deposits and the known reserves of "OPEC" Venezuela. Oil spills present a problem but much research is being done on the fate of oil spills in the

marine environment and mitigation of spills if they
occur.

4

Extracting Energy From the Ocean

Bernard Le Mehaute

A storm of gigantic proportions is pounding our United States coastlines. This storm is not the result of an extreme meteorological event, but it will be with us for a long time. It is the result of the political and legal fights to determine which areas should be converted into industrial complexes, recreational resorts, or kept in their pristine state.

The fact that the shoreline is under stress is an understatement. It is forecast that more than 60 percent of Americans will live near the coastal water by 1985.

Point Conception, California, is a typical example of the dilemma. One can understand why the people who live on Hollister Ranch want to prevent the construction of a liquefied natural gas (LNG) terminal at Cojo. On the other hand, there are 7 million people in Los Angeles who need gas, energy, and jobs.

And the pressure remains: from the population to live closer to the beach, from the industries to have access to the sea for myriads of technical and economic reasons.

The solutions are complex and will not satisfy every group.

Bernard Le Mehaute is Professor and Head of Ocean Engineering, Rosenstiel School of Oceanography, University of Miami, Florida. Formerly he was Senior Vice President, Tetra Tech, Inc. Pasadena, California. Dr. Le Mehaute is an authority on ocean engineering and coastal processes and the author of numerous works on ocean engineering.

It is the function of the engineer to bring to light technological and scientific facts and numbers, as much as possible in such a way that the economists, the politicians, and the population at large are allowed to make a choice "en connaissance de cause."

From an engineering point of view, the problems facing coastal development and preservation are multiple. The loss of real estate value by shoreline erosion amounts to billions of dollars each year. The delay in construction of superports --Loop in Louisiana is finally being done--and the legislative process which is needed to establish any kind of job-producing industries along our shorelines are dragging our productivity and the economy.

I will limit my discussion to water and energy. I will examine water, and in particular, ocean water, as a source of power and water usage in energy production. I will also survey the subsequent problems which are created and the ultimate solutions.

In the past, dependence on food and energy production on the availability of water was localized, but today, this dependence is so strong that an integrated approach is absolutely necessary. Water needs vary from region to region. Globally, if one takes into account variations in specific consumption due to domestic, agricultural, and industrial needs, one estimates that there is enough land and fresh water on earth to sustain a population of 30 billion people. The North American continent can provide a comfortable 1020 cubic kilometers of water per year per capita to 1,145 million people.

The degree of interdependence among water, food, and energy varies over the world from countries such as Canada, with its small density of population and vast water resources, to countries of the Middle East, where water is a most precious commodity.

In many of the United States, the water consumption and future demand already exceed the local supply, and the future energy demand reinforces the problem. In general, the country is water-rich east of the Mississippi River and water-poor to its west with the exception of the water-abundant Pacific Northwest. But even within the water-rich regions, there are localized supply problems.

The Boston-Washington megalopolis and parts of Florida are examples. From an overall standpoint,

52

however, the East is not as seriously constrained by its lack of water supply as the environmental problems besetting it. "Water, taken in moderation, never hurt anybody," said Mark Twain. Today's reality is, "Water used in immoderation hurts everybody."

Problems associated with water usage are critical worldwide. These problems, however, are solvable. The solutions to these problems do not require new breakthroughs in technology, but rather new approaches in technical management and a clear understanding between the fundamental relationship between the ocean's water and energy requirements.

Water is essential in all human and industrial functions. It takes, for example, 20,000 gallons of water to produce the steel for one car and 10,000 gallons for the car's assembly. Also, much more water is needed for food and energy production.

For thousands of years, man has recognized, sometimes only dimly and sometimes clearly, that water moves in a continuous self-purifying cycle. This is the cycle that begins when rain falls from clouds, sinks into the earth, seeps into rivers, lakes and oceans, then evaporates into the atmosphere to begin the cycle all over again. In one vitally important respect, water's behavior is steadfast; the world's supply of water neither grows nor diminishes. It is believed to be the same now as it was three billion years ago.

The oceans, ice caps, and glaciers contribute 99.35 percent of the earth's water. The small remainder accounts for all the earth's rivers, lakes, and underground water tables. Yet it is this small amount that we use every day in myriad ways.

About 517 trillion metric tons (equivalent to a volume of 124,000 cubic miles of water) evaporates into the atmosphere annually. A far greater part, about 88 percent rises from the ocean. Twelve percent is drawn from the land, evaporated from lakes, rivers, streams, etc. Of the water that goes into the atmosphere, 79 percent falls back directly into the oceans. Another 21 percent falls on the land, but 9 percent runs off into the rivers and streams and is returned to the oceans within days. The remaining 12 percent soaks into the land and is available for plant and animal life processes.

In these processes, too, water intake matches output, as animal and vegetable life exhales, exhales, excretes, and perspires what was earlier ingested through root and mouth. In a sense, the world's water circulation system operates like a

53

complex, gigantic pump driven by solar energy. Endlessly, recycled water is used, disposed of, purified and used again by nature including humans. The coffee that you drink at noon may have been made of what was, ages ago, the bath water of Archimedes. Past, current, and projected growth of the world's population with its huge demands for energy and food has affected and will profoundly affect this natural cycle in terms of biological, chemical, and thermal waste (while chemical waste can be processed, thermal waste cannot).

The increasing demand for water supply will come from the increasing demand for energy production and food supply. Both are dependent upon energy availability.

The first form of energy extracted from the water element is hydropower. Hydropower has not been given the proper attention in view of our energy shortage. It is a nonpolluting form of energy. There are still huge amounts of power readily available which could be obtained by harnessing rivers and tidal embayments even in the United States.

The United States has the potential to quadruple its production of energy from hydropower--not counting energy-rich Alaska. The U.S. Army Corps of Engineers has identified 49,500 existing dams which could potentially be considered for hydropower production. Three thousand of these dams are in energy-poor New Hampshire. Some of them were used in the past for hydropower, but their operation was stopped as being noncompetitive in an oil-cheap era. The harnessing of many of these installations would be economical and should not create any environmental impact, since the dams are already built.

The potential for new hydropower installations is also significant. The economic problem sometimes arises from transporting the energy from the center of production to the center of consumption. A few worldwide examples are:

--The Inga Project, considered in 1950, consisted of the harnessing the natural fall of the Congo River with 300 turbines of 200 megawatts each. This would then be transported to Europe through 400,000 volt D.C. lines.
--The torrents of the Himalaya Mountains are practically in pristine state; mere penstocks and Pelton turbines can provide India with all its needed energy. But the mountains are in the North and the centers of consumption are

in the South. Nevertheless, is there any need
for India to resort to nuclear power and discard hydropower so easily?

--Tidal power availability at San Jose, Argen-
tina, is practically unlimited. The center of
consumption is Buenos Aires, further North.

--In the United States, a tidal power project at
Cook Inlet can provide us with 75.000 million
kilowatt hours per year, while the demand in
Alaska is only 1.200. It is about 3 percent
of the total U.S. electrical production and 1
percent of the total U.S. energy consumption.

I would not like to speculate, at this time,
on a possible breakthrough in energy transportation
(superconductors, transmission of hydrogen, etc.),
but if it were to happen, these projects and many
others of this type would become immediately
viable. Let us now survey the ocean as a potential
source of energy.

Ocean as Source of Energy

The amount of energy potential available in
the sea, both visible and invisible, is practically
limitless and thermally nonpolluting. Some of the
estimates of this energy are truly staggering:

--25 billion kilowatt of energy is constantly
being dissipated along the world's shorelines
by waves. A surface wave three meters high
with constant period and amplitude transmits
100 kilowatts for every meter of wave crest of
100 megawatts per kilometer (assuming that the
wave period is 11.3 seconds). It could be compared to the power of a line of automobiles,
side by side, at full throttle. Tides could
be harnessed to produce 1,240 billion kilowatt
hours per year.

--The Gulf stream off Florida has a volume flow
of over fifty times the total discharge of all
the rivers of the world.
--Enough electricity could be generated from
heat engines operated on the temperature differential between surface and deeper ocean
waters to provide more than 10,000 times the
world's yearly electric power requirements.

--The salinity power represented by the osmotic
pressure between fresh water and salt water is
equivalent to a waterfall of 700 feet. From

the global runoff of fresh water into the oceans, 2.6 billion kilowatt of power can potentially be obtained.

Energy from the ocean has many forms. There is enough solar energy to maintain the entire world population at an affluent level, but it is a diffused form providing at best 100 watts per square foot in full sunlight. Some means for collection this energy must therefore be found.

Wind power is one form which has been the major source of energy used for ocean transportation until the invention of the heat engine. Windmills are also extensively used at special sites, but a steady velocity of thirty to forty knots is required for the economic generation of energy. The worst place to install a wind power generator is at sea despite stronger prevailing winds. On land, about one-third of the cost is the tower, two-thirds the propeller and the auxiliaries. At sea, the supporting structures must not only stand the wind force but also the wave force, so increasing its cost by an order of magnitude. The cost of transporting the energy from the sea to the centers of consumption is also added to its lack of economic attractiveness.

In order for an energy production system to be worth developing, it must satisfy a number of criteria. Three of them are: 1) it must use a high energy density medium; 2) it must have a simple processing method; and 3) it must use a source of energy which is dependable.

The energy density is directly related to the volume to be processed and to the size of the machinery which is needed to extract the energy from that medium. Therefore, the cost is related to energy density.

For example, oil is a high-energy density medium. When one deals with hydropower, the energy density is proportional to the head: the higher the head, the cheaper the energy. One of the cheapest forms of energy is the one provided by the water power coming from mountains through narrow penstocks and ejectors and splashing the buckets of a simple Pelton turbine. As the head decreases, there is a limit which is considered economically unattractive. When the head is below, say two meters, even a small turbine built to satisfy local needs could not be considered economical.

By the same token, one can disregard a priori all the energy which is contained in large currents such as the Gulf Stream. Typically, the speed of the Gulf Stream is 0.6 to 2 m/sec, the corresponding maximum head is twenty centimeters. It can, in no case, enter the realm of economic expectations.

The total amount of power available in water wave is also huge, but it is very diffused. The energy density (i.e., per unit of volume at the free surface) or equivalent head is so small that it can only be considered for local and special purposes as buoys and in isolated areas.

The place of the tidal power in terms of energy density is easy to assess: the head is linearly related to the tidal amplitude and the energy available is proportional to its square. Even the largest tidal heads are generally at the lower limit of what should be considered economical. Therefore, tidal power in general is a marginal form of energy to be considered at special sites with narrow bay entrances (to limit the cost of dike construction).

The million-kw Passamaquoddy project in the Bay of Fundy would cost 3 billion dollars nowadays because of the length of the dikes. But a small, entirely U.S. project at Cobscook Bay will be economical because of its narrow entrance, based on a forecast of increase of fossil fuel energy.

The processing methodology has a significant impact on cost. The simpler it is, the least capital cost and the least maintenance cost. The transformation of water power energy into mechanical and electrical energy is relatively simple. It is a very effective process. The efficiency of a hydraulic turbine is as high as 96 percent. Water power is one of the simplest energy process conversions which exist, as opposed to thermal, chemical, or nuclear conversion.

The energy density over a thermal gradient is very large. Each $1^{\circ}C$ of temperature difference corresponds to an equivalent head of 426 meters, implying a potentially high energy density. The problem is processing.

The ocean thermal energy conversion is presently considered with great optimism by many. The earth's oceans can be viewed as natural thermal collectors and storage devices. At 1,500 feet below sea level, the water temperature is close to the freezing point and on the surface, the water temperature in tropical regions range between $70-85^{\circ}F$. These temperature differences cause density stratification that retards fluid mixing and prevents the ocean from arriving at a uniform temperature. The existence of the temperature gradient in principle can be tapped to run heat engines, to generate electricity or hydrogen.

The thermodynamic efficiency of ocean thermal energy conversion (OTEC) power plants is controlled by the available ocean water temperature differential, efficiency of the heat exchangers, fluid energy losses from pumping large amounts of water, and frictional losses incurred by the power plant machinery. An overall efficiency of between 2 to 3 percent, typical for such plants, is governed principally by the Carnot efficiency. This astonishingly low efficiency does not preclude its viability, however, since the fuel, in this case seawater, is free. But the processing methodology requires a huge amount of liquid to be circulated through a heat exchanger. For this reason, there is very little hope that this process may become economical in the near future, but its cost may become competitive if the cost of fossil fuels continue to escalate. Nevertheless, it will take many years of OTEC energy just to produce enough energy to construct an OTEC platform. However, significant improvements in the heat transfer surface technology could make the OTEC concept appear in a more favorable light. The cost of thirty mills per kilowatt hours has been presented as feasible.

The benefit of the present OTEC project is multiple. The technology fallout in ocean engineering as the result of the research presently being done could be significant. For example, there is some hope that interesting solutions can be found for biofouling control, deepsea mooring, construction of large structures, and special shipyard development. The Department of Defense may also benefit from such a project since the OTEC platform goes deep into the sound channel. But there is very little hope in the near future that the banks will loan money to a utility company or the stockholders invest capital to build an OTEC platform. The total power generated by OTEC, like tidal power, will remain very small in terms of world energy demand. Our effort should be pursued, but our expectation realistic: at most 1 percent of our energy supply by the year 2000.

The same consideration applies for energy from osmotic pressure generated by the mixing of fresh water with seawater. This amount of energy is also huge. The head is 700 feet. The scheme to recover this energy is relatively simple, since it is sufficient to build an underground water power plant at the mouth of rivers and to connect the tailgate

58

tunnel with a network of underwater osmotic membranes spreading the freshwater in the ocean. The problem is then that the area of membranes per unit of fluid discharge is so large that it does not appear economically feasible. However, basic scientific research in this field should be pursued at a moderate rate of expense.

Therefore, from all the sources of energy available in the oceans, tidal power is the one which necessitates the simplest processing method. It is to be expected that the wear and fatigue of other sources of energy at sea such as wave power or thermal gradient will be such that their lifetime may be shorter since they are exposed to the violence of the oceanic elements. On the other hand, tidal power installations are to be built in well-protected areas. Tidal power once installed could still be there centuries from now. Some old tidal mills, built centuries ago, still exist in Europe. France, the USSR, and China have tidal power plants and others are being planned in Korea and Canada.

Dependability Required

Finally, the source of energy must be dependable. Oceanic thermal gradient and osmotic pressure energy from rivers arriving into the oceans are dependable sources of energy. The recovery of energy from wave power has always fascinated inventors, but it is not dependable. R. Dhaille reports (1965) that he examined more than 600 patents, some of them demonstrating a disarming ignorance of the laws of physics. He concluded that not even one was worth developing. More than eighty years ago, Albert Stahl cited twenty proposals for harnessing wave power in the United States. The back-and-forth motion of breaking waves and at times their devastating effects may give the impression that a huge amount of energy could be tapped.

The main economic problem arises because any structure has to be designed to withstand the largest storm waves, while the prevailing waves, which would provide most of the energy, are smaller by an order of magnitude. Finally, wind-generated waves are not a dependable source of energy as a result of the large variation of sea states inherent to meteorological fluctuations.

Along the U.S. Pacific Coast, the 100 kw/m is exceeded only 1 percent of the time at most locations, and 2.5 kw/m is exceeded 80 percent of the time.

The most ambitious project now being considered for recovering wave power is located ten miles west of the Hebrides Islands off the coast of Scotland. The proposed device would be a series of axles each with twenty to forty huge swiveling cams. Each set would be as long as a supertanker. The set of cams will then be a few hundred kilometers long.

The up and down wave-induced motion pumps water to a high level. The corresponding potential energy is then processed through a turbine generator or is used to generate hydrogen. Each cam unit would cost $48 million and produce fifty megawatts based on the severe nature of the sea states in this part of the world. Its promoter considers wave power as the ultimate clean solution to the electrical requirements of the United Kingdom. Whether this optimistic assessment will be substantiated by the facts remains open.

On the other hand, tidal power is extremely dependable, since the tidal amplitude can be predicted as far ahead as needed as a function of trajectories of celestial bodies. Still, tidal power fluctuates substantially from the equinox to the solstice and from day to day. More importantly, the sea level varies continously with time. But there are ways to cope with that variation, in such a way that one can produce the energy at the time it is required. In this respect, tidal power is very dependable. It has been said that tidal power varies with the moon when the life on earth is regulated according to the sun. Actually, by various schemes, it is possible to extract power at any time one wants, either a peak power or almost steady production, and to depend upon the general network to which tidal power is connected with for coping with the problem of tidal fluctuations. In this respect, the tidal power can be classified as one of the most dependable forms of energy, even more dependable than water power from rivers, since floods and dry periods are to some extent also unpredictable.

There is very little maintenance to be done once the plant is built. The relatively large capital cost which is required initially has to be balanced by the fact that after it is built, it will be there practically forever (a thermal or nuclear power plant has a thirty-year lifetime). But the United States has very few sites which could be harnessed economically.

As one can see, there is very little hope that "Project Independence" could be achieved from energy sources for the water element alone. Let us now examine our need for water and, to begin with, the demand that other energy sources create for water.

Demand for Water From Other Energy Sources

In the United States, most energy processes are dependent on uses of water . (By contrast, in the Middle Eastern countries, most water problems are dependent upon uses of energy.) Oil, natural gas, coal, oil shale, synthetic fuels, geothermal, and nuclear power are all energy sources which need water.

Oil and natural gas both require water for drilling. Wherever secondary or tertiary recovery techniques are used, however, much larger amounts of water are necessary, since vast amounts must be pumped underground to force the underlying oil or gas to the surface. Since the United States consumes approximately seventeen gallons of water for each barrel of oil produced, water is intimately related to these forms of energy production.

Coal mining consumes water for several purposes. Access roads and coal surfaces being worked must be watered down for dust control in both surface and underground mines. Water is also used to wash the mined coal, transport the coal away from the mine in slurry form through pipelines, wash up by mine personnel and to help in revegetation of stripmined areas. The amount of water consumed varies from four to eighteen gallons per ton of coal mined, depending on the region. Water withdrawals also vary among regions from as little as four gallons to as much as 430 gallons per ton. The water requirement of coal conversion plants is not large, even in the semiarid west, compared with the quantities devoted to irrigation. (A coal refinery processing 75,000 tons of coal per day would need 15 million gallons of water per day. This comes out to about 15,000 acre-feet per year). But a supply of water, like a supply of coal, must clearly be taken into consideration for each plant.

Extracting crude oil from shale with presently available technology requires large amounts of water. First of all, water is necessary in the mining and processing of the shale. Second, the oil present after retorting (distilling by heat and pressure in the presence of a catalyst) is of such

61

high viscosity that a hydro-cracking process is necessary to upgrade the shale oil into a useful fuel. Finally, more water is needed to compact and stabilize the spent shale and to control dust. Besides these industrial uses, additional water for personal household use and related industrial uses will be required if any significant development of oil shale resources is undertaken--since large numbers of workers would have to be imported into the now sparsely populated areas of potential oil shale production. Research indicates that a plant producing 100,000 barrels of oil a day will require 16,800 acre-feet of water each year.

Water quality requirements for shale oil vary. Higher quality water is necessary for retorting and upgrading the shale oil and for household use by the industrial workers to be imported into the area. But spend shale disposal can be accomplished with brackish or other lower quality waters. This might be obtained from dewatering the shale mines.

Producing synthetic fuels from coal consumes water in three ways. First, water is used in the chemical processes that convert the coal into gas or liquid fuel. Second, water is evaporated in the cooling activities associated with these processes. Third, water leaves the processing site as moisture content in the coal ash and waste discharges. Consumptive use ranges from less than ten gallons per million BTUs for the liquid and Fischer-Tropsch processes (that produce hydrocarbons and their derivatives) to over 100 gallons per million BTUs for those processes that produce pipeline gas. Research indicates a plant capable of providing 100,000 barrels of synthetic oil daily consumes over 5,900 acre feet of water a year.

Geothermal water requirements for a plant using the hot water technology would be very small, probably no more than 470 acre-feet a year for a 200 megawatt (MWe) plant. There are no forseeable water requirements for the dry steam design, since the hot dry rock technology may or may not use water as its fluid.

Nuclear power generation withdrawal and consumption requirements are derived essentially for cooling needs. Nuclear plant water consumption factors vary with the type of plant and cooling processes used. In general, a water consumption factor of 0.8 gallons per kilowatt hour is needed. The mining and processing of the raw fuel--uranium ore --also requires the use of some water.

Our vast requirements for electrical power depend totally on the availability of cooling water from our lakes, rivers, and coastal zones. Indeed, if one excludes hydropower, which is thermally non-polluting, the purpose of all energy sources (fossil fuel, geothermal, or nuclear) is to create a high temperature, T_1. In order to obtain consumable energy, a lower temperature, T_2, is also needed. The availability of cooling water is as important as the heat source. If there is a large resource of energy at sea, it is "T_2," while the heat capacity is very great compared to that of other substances. It is that property that allows the California current to moderate the climate on the California coast, and which also keeps the earth's surface at a relatively constant temperature.

Nevertheless, the problem of waste heat will be with us forever. The technological change in power generation cannot be expected to solve this problem for us. The United States consumes 7.3 trillion kilowatt hours a year, close to 35 percent of the world's energy consumption. Of this total, the vast majority comes from three fossil fuels: petroleum, natural gas, and coal. Together, these fuels represent more than 90 percent of the U.S. energy supply. Coal (with its important demands on freshwater for processing) and nuclear power will begin to increase their share of the energy supply from now to the end of the century, with more exotic energy forms contributing in a minor way.

Ultimately, all this energy consumed ends up as heat and increases T_2. Energy sources such as petroleum would not have contributed to the production of heat if it had not been consumed. The same will apply to nuclear energy, coal, etc. (water, tidal, wind and solar power result in no net increase in heat). Thermal pollution has been presented as the ultimate limit to energy development. Indeed, the problem of thermal waste deserves the most attention, because heat is the ultimate residual of society's activities, and the only one which cannot be processed. Any effort to concentrate it simply requires more energy compounding the waste heat.

On a local basis, the total waste heat released is substantial (for example, about 5 percent of solar radiation in Los Angeles). The total perturbation, on a global basis due to man's energy input, is small compared to the global heat budget (0.01 percent of insulation at the surface). The amount of energy received by the earth, by solar energy, and the one which radiates is by orders of magnitude larger than the human made perturbation. Ultimately, the excess heat is diffused in the ocean, the atmosphere, and finally radiated to space. For this reason, the sea should be considered as a sink of almost infinite recycling capability. Thermal pollution problems are only of local nature and can be solved by the proper disposal and spreading. By contrast with the shoreline which is unidimensional, the land which is two-dimensional, the sea is four-dimensional, and it has not only the two horizontal dimensions but also depth, and it "stirs," adding a time-space relationship permitting heat diffusion and absorption of higher concentrations of foreign elements.

For every square mile of land, there are 2.5 square miles of ocean, five times deeper than land is high. On must consider our largest continents as islands.

For a moment, let us be energy optimists; that is, let us assume that the energy supply is practically limitless (and present technology--the breeder reactor--permits us to consider that it is already practically limitless). Then what would be the limit to the use of energy caused by thermal pollution? The total heat loss of the atmosphere to space, initially received from the sun, is about 100,000 billion kilowatts. Man-created heat is about 5 billion kilowatt (i.e., five divided by 100,000 of the sun's contribution).

Let us assume for a while that the earth's population has grown to 10 billion, all of them consuming 20 kilowatts/ person. (The U.S. consumption is 10 kilowatts). Then the total man-made heat will be 200 billion kilowatts (400 times the present) it still will be only 0.2 percent of the earth's natural rate of heat loss. This would increase the earth temperature by less than $1/10^\circ$C. Thus, the total heat balance will hardly be affected since temperature variation of 2°C or more have been recorded in the past. Therefore, on a global scale, the limit to the use of energy because of thermal pollution is at quite a distance even if the results of the previous calculations are erroneous by an order of magnitude. On a short-term basis, thermal "pollution" may be considered as one of the great untapped resources of our oceans since fish farming is much more efficient in warmer water. Since the limit to the use of energy is quite large, the limit to the use of water is also very comfortable.

64

A Potential Reservoir for Protein

The sea is not only the ultimate sink, but it is also the ultimate source. The present need for water as required for energy production is and will be compounded by the need for agriculture, irrigation, and land reclamation.

An estimated 1,600 million persons are starving and every year close to 100 million more have to be fed. For this, many look at the sea as a potential reservoir of protein, and even though much progress has been made in mariculture and aquaculture, this effort still has a minimum impact. Except for oysters and shrimp, aquaculture is more experimental than operational.

New trawler designs and equipment have created a revolution in fisheries, increasing the catch by an order of magnitude, but unfortunately leading to a depletion of school populations. Therefore, the ultimate solution, in addition to fisheries management, is desalinization, irrigation of arid land, and fertilizer plants (which in turn require more energy).

It takes about one kilowatt per hour of work to separate 100 pounds of salt from 300 gallons of water. One presently estimates that this process will cost at most 30 C in terms of energy. The cost of water in Israel is three C/100 gallons.

Is it worth that cost?

One estimates that 700 M^2 of irrigated land are needed for each person, requiring as an average 500 liters/day or about 150 gallons of water. These 700 m^2 of irrigated land provide enough crops for insuring the daily requirement of 2,500 calories per capita. If one adds the cost of the conveyance system, which may actually triple the cost, it means that about ten c of water/day/man will permit all of humanity to live in good health.

Water is cheap: 100 times cheaper than food, and a significant increase in the cost of water is not going to have much effect on inflation or the economy, but its availability and the availability of energy can effectvely insure us of a better world. Inversely, energy is needed for desalinization but in an acceptable amount.

One can conclude that on a long-term basis, given a limitless energy source, such as due to hydrogen fusion or breeder reactors, the T_2 of the ocean permits us to produce a practically limitless amount of energy, which in turn permits us to obtain a limitless amount of water for cultivation of our arid land.

I would like to conclude not that the world population can keep growing or even that we can accept thermal pollution without further concern, monitoring, and eventually control, but that a priori water, energy, and even food are not the reasons to limit the expansion of humanity. The problem is not technological but economic and managerial at a world scale.

The problem is a matter of resources management. One could say that there cannot be, there will never be, a water shortage as such. But there may be a shortage of water transmission systems, water-treatment plants, water-storage reservoirs, or more generally, engineering construction. There may be a shortage of capital, skills, ingenuity, resourcefulness, creativity, and a national will. There certainly may be a shortage of enlightened management. America is like an ostrich with its head in the sand where water and energy matters are concerned. The water problem is basically a management problem, not a technical one, and as a large part of management is the environmental and sociocultural context for our future generation.

I recently read that "undue faith in technology has created a completely unrealistic sense of the limitness of the resources," meaning water. I will state instead, "faith in technology, human inventiveness, and creativity permits us to consider that, given time and enlightened leadership, water and energy are indeed limitless resources, and these resources are ultimately in our oceans."

5

Conducting Ocean Science From Space

Robert F. Hummer

Does studying oceanography from outer space make any sense? What is "remote sensing" and why does it have to be so remote? What properties of the oceans can be measured remotely? How are they measured? What does the future hold?

Before attempting to answer these questions I would like to discuss meteorology because oceanography and meteorology have much in common. At the sea-air interface vast amounts of latent energy are transferred from the sun-heated sea to the atmosphere. In its kinetic form this energy pumps the global circulation of the atmosphere and gives rise to weather. Weather in turn interacts with the ocean and its processes. Understanding the oceans, like understanding the weather, requires a grand-scale view of vast dynamic happenings.

Early Weather Prediction

In the 1930's research meteorologists realized that the best way to predict weather was to establish a numerical model, a set of mathematical equations, describing the dynamic circulation of the earth's atmosphere. By introducing into this model today's weather parameters, such as wind, temperature, pressure, and humidity, they might be able to predict next week's weather. Much theoretical work was done in establishing the complex equations for modeling, however, it was soon realized that to test

Robert Hummer is Manager of Electro-Optical Systems, Santa Barbara Research Center, Santa Barbara, California, and an authority on spacecraft optical systems.

the model, refine it, and make it operational a great many observations would be needed around the world. Since weather is such a dynamic phenomenon these observations would have to be made at nearly the same time, certainly within the span of a few hours.

In developed nations there were networks of weather stations reporting to regional and national centers. Elsewhere data were sparse, particularly over the oceans where weather really originates. Thus, progress in developing circulation models of the atmosphere was hampered by the lack of correlated input.

In 1960 this situation changed dramatically with the launch of the first weather satellite, the Television Infared Observational Satellite (TIROS). This 515-mile high satellite circling the earth every 100 minutes in polar orbit was able to photography the entire globe every thirteen hours. Not only did meteorologists now have an eye in the sky that could synoptically monitor the large-scale motions of the atmosphere; but of equal importance, the meteorological data were internally consistent because the same instruments were used to measure the global parameters. A far cry from the sprinkling of ground observers whose measuring instruments were of sometimes uncertain accuracy.

Improvements Since 1960

Tremendous strides have been made since 1960 in the quality and range of measurements possible from meteorological satellites. In 1979, the first experiments of the Global Atmospheric Research Project will focus the full power of this technology in a worldwide undertaking for the good of all mankind.

Similar technology can be applied to the numerical modeling of the physical and biological systems in the ocean. Because of the complex interaction of many ocean processes, this is a particularly challenging task. Not only do the oceans cover most of the planet, but within them and on their surfaces large-scale changes take place in a short time. Thus the oceanographer is faced with the familiar problem that numerical models, to be useful, must be fed detailed large-scale sequential data. With suitable sensors a space platform can synoptically monitor the motion, temperatures, and other related parameters of the oceans with sufficient spatial

68

and temporal resolution to support numerical models which will in turn allow new depths of understanding of regional and worldwide trends.

The National Aeronautics and Space Administration (NASA) has established the Oceanography and Marine Resources Program to apply high technology developments of the space program to the problems of the oceans and coastal zones. The major goals of this program are shown in Table 5.1. These goals are generally concerned with the productivity of the oceans and coastal zones, and with natural phenomena and man's activities that directly or indirectly preserve, alter, destroy, or enhance the resources of the open ocean or coastal areas.

Successful achievement of these goals requires that we be able to identify, measure, and analyze a number of parameters and processes that operate or react together in a highly dynamic environment. If we look at a representative list of such parameters (Table 5.2) we see that some are quite obvious, but others have more subtle implications. Ice monitoring is obvious; we want to keep the shipping lanes open or we want to know where the open shipping lanes are. This is particularly important in the shear fields off Northern Canada and Northern Alaska. Therefore, it is necessary to view and to track the ice fields on a large-scale, time-repetitive basis. Also, the oceanographer wants to better understand the dynamics and morphology of the ice fields by observing their formation and movements.

Temperature is a very important parameter to measure on a global and regional basis because it is an indicator of currents and a locator of water masses. Also, it is a measure of the heat energy transferred across the land-sea and sea-air interfaces. This energy drives the great global heat engine that circulates the atmosphere and gives rise to weather.

Current is important because it is an indicator of wind which is a driving force for the surface circulation of the oceans. Sea state is an indication of the wind stress at the surface of the sea and thus related to the energy exchange at the sea surface.

Suspended sediment is a good tracer for currents showing the coastal circulation in particular. Surface slicks and films are again tracers of current indicating boundaries and fronts in the ocean.

Oceanographers are interested in the ocean surface topography, the so-called geoid, because

TABLE 5.1 NASA Oceanography and Marine Resources Program

DEVELOP REMOTE SENSING TECHNOLOGY TO ASSIST IN:

● EFFICIENT MANAGEMENT OF LIVING MARINE RESOURCES

● EFFECTIVE MANAGEMENT OF COASTAL ZONE ACTIVITIES

● EFFECTIVE USE OF OCEAN TRANSPORTATION ROUTES

● ADVANCEMENT OF MARINE BIOLOGY AND OCEANOGRAPHY

Source: Author

TABLE 5.2
Parameters and Processes to be Measured

- PHYSICAL AND METEOROLOGICAL:
    - ICE
    - TEMPERATURE
    - CURRENT
    - SEA/AIR INTERACTION
    - SEA STATE
    - SUSPENDED SEDIMENT
    - SURFACE SLICKS AND FILMS
- GEOMETRIC:
    - OCEAN SURFACE TOPOGRAPHY
    - LAND/SEA INTERFACE
    - BATHYMETRY
- OPTICAL:
    - WATER COLOR
    - BOTTOM COLOR
- CHEMICAL:
    - SALINITY
    - CHLOROPHYLL
    - POLLUTANTS
- BIOLOGICAL:
    - PLANTS
    - ANIMALS

Source: Author

dips and trenches in the ocean bottom affect the level of the gravitational equipotential surface above. The land-sea interface is important from the standpoint of geological processes. Bathymetry is depth determination and also of interest in understanding coastal processes.

Water color can indicate the presence of plants, chlorophyll, plankton, and biological activity in general. Bottom color is sometimes useful in determining the depth of water.

Salinity will be a very difficult parameter to measure from space. It is important as an identifier for water masses and a tracer for water mass movement. Pollutants, of course, are important to measure and trace.

Mapping the distribution and quantity of plants and animals will aid the new science of aquaculture and will help predict future catches of commercial and sport fish species.

Meaning of Remote Sensing

Before discussing how these measurements will be made from an orbiting platform hundreds of miles above the ocean's surface, I would like to define "remote sensing" and describe the types of sensors available for these measurements. The dictionary defines remote sensing as "the acquisition of physical data of an object without touch or contact." As generally used, "remote sensing" refers to the recording and analysis of electromagnetic radiation (emr)--visible light, infrared heat radiation, radio waves, and similar forms of wave-transmitted energy. These waves have a common velocity, the speed of light at 186,000-miles per second, but the wavelength varies from one millionth of a meter for gamma rays to many miles for long wavelength radio. The human eye is only sensitive to an infinitesimal fraction of the total emr spectrum, but imaging systems that respond to emr within the spectral response range of the eye have had a long and productive history of development since the first photographs of the 1830's. Although the existence of emr adjacent to the blue region of the visible spectrum (ultraviolet) and adjacent to the red (infrared) were demonstrated over 170 years ago, nearly all useful applications of these regions have taken place only over the past forty years; principally because of technological breakthroughs at the time of World War II.

72

Remote-sensing of the earth from space is limited to relatively narrow portions of the visible, infrared, and microwave radio spectrums. The gases in the atmosphere selectively absorb certain spectral components of incoming sunlight, and similarly absorb components of outgoing radiation. Only spectral regions in which the atmosphere is non-absorbing, the so-called "atmospheric windows," are useful in remote sensing from outside the atmosphere.

Every object at temperature above absolute zero (450°F) emits electromagnetic radiation because of the motion of its molecules. Objects near standard room temperature, 68°F, radiate in the infrared at a wavelength of approximately 10 millionths of a meter. Fortunately, a very clear atmospheric window exists at this wavelength, and most remote sensors for mearsuring the radiation temperature of the oceans and land operate within this window.

Figure 5.1 shows schematically how reflected sunlight and self-emitted heat radiation due to molecular action reach the satellite and are recorded. There are many paths possible for reflected sunlight: direct reflection both specular (mirror-like) from calm water and diffuse from clouds, waves, land, and molecular scattering within the atmosphere. Emitted radiation is more direct but suffers some scattering and absorption in the atmosphere.

Representative types of spaceborne sensors are listed in Table 5.3. The film camera has been limited to manned space missions where the film can be returned to earth for processing. All other sensors generate electrical signals which are transmitted to earth and converted into images. The image tube, a generic name for various types of television sensors, was the first extensively used in space. For various technical reasons it has been superseded by the multispectral scanner which, as the name implies, can view the earth at a few wavelengths simultaneously with excellent registration of the color images.

The infrared radiometer is a device for measuring the radiation temperature of the terrain, clouds, and sea surface. Absolute temperature accuracy of one degree centrigrade is not uncommon.

The infrared spectrometer is a sensor for viewing the scene at a great number of wavelength intervals at the same time. Absolute radiometric accuracy may not be high, but there will be good relative accuracy from color to color. It is

FIGURE 5.1 Solar-Thermal Radiative Interactions

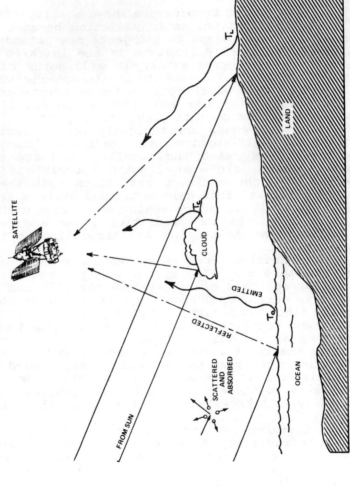

Source: Santa Barbara Research Center

TABLE 5.3

Spaceborne Remote Sensors

PASSIVE:

   FILM CAMERA

   IMAGE TUBE

   MULTISPECTRAL SCANNER

   INFRARED RADIOMETER

   INFRARED SPECTROMETER

   MICROWAVE RADIOMETER

ACTIVE:

   IMAGING RADAR

   RADAR ALTIMETER

   SCATTEROMETER

   LASER RADAR

Source: Santa Barbara Research Center

principally a research tool used in exploratory survey of the spectrum to determine, for example, what trace gases might be in the atmosphere at a particular time and place.

The microwave radiometer is much like the infrared radiometer, but operates in the microwave radio spectrum where there are a number of transparent regions in the atmosphere. In fact, at some wavelengths within this spectrum radiation can actually penetrate clouds and rain. The microwave radiometer does not have the high spatial resolution nor the temperature accuracy of the infrared radiometer, but it does have an all-weather capability. On the average, 60 percent of the world's ocean surface is covered by clouds; therefore, the microwave radiometer has a distinct operational advantage.

The sensors discussed so far are passive, i.e., they sense reflected sunlight and self-emitted infrared radiation from the oceans, clouds, and terrain. A second class of sensor, radar, is in the early stages of application from space platforms. Radar generates its own radiation, its own light. Some radars send out pulses of radio frequency radiation which are reflected from the ground or wave tops. A portion of this reflected energy is returned to the radar's receiving antenna. Since these pulses are traveling at the speed of light and can be accurately timed from transmission to reception, the distance to the object being "illuminated" is known. Also, the pulses travel in a very narrow beam which can be steered in any direction by moving the radar antenna. Radar, in fact, is the acronym for radio direction and ranging.

A radar altimeter beams its pulses directly down from the spacecraft, along the nadir; timing the pulse return echos yields the altitude of the satellite above the radar-reflecting ocean surface. An earth-orbiting satellite free from any external forces other than the gravitational attraction of earth travels in a precisely determined orbit. Once the initial orbital parameters are set the position of the satellite at any time (its emphemeris) is known to a few centimeters. Therefore, radar altimeter readings from orbit enable oceanographers to determine the geoid or gravitational equipotential surface of the ocean.

The scatterometer is a useful device for determining the roughness of the ocean by measuring radar returns scattered off the waves. The scatterometer tells the direction and amplitude of the waves and, therefore, the sea state. Laser radar is simply a radar in which light energy rather than microwave energy is bounced off the surface of the ocean or land.

Figure 5.2 illustrates how the earth is scanned by electronic sensors aboard a spacecraft. The motion of the spacecraft along its orbit produces one dimension of scan, the so-called along-track component; the field of view of passive sensors and the radar beam of active sensors are caused to move from side to side, across-track, to form the second dimension of the image.

LANDSAT Capability

Probably the best-known earth imaging satellite is LANDSAT, which has returned over 400,000 highly detailed color images. LANDSAT orbits the earth at an altitude of 560 miles circling the globe over the poles every 103 minutes. The ground speed, to use aircraft terminology, is 14,500 miles per hour. A Multispectral Scanner in a high-speed crosstrack scan mode images the earth in five color bands of the visible and infrared spectrum. A continuous strip image 115 miles wide is transmitted by electrical pulses to ground receiving stations where the images are reconstructed. Because of the speed of the satellite and the high information content of the images, the picture pulses from the scanner arrive at earth at the astounding rate of 15,000,000 per second! An improved scanner, the Thematic Mapper, being developed for a future LANDSAT, will generate picture pulses at the rate of 90 million per second.

Referring again to Figure 5.2, the orbital plane of the satellite is always pointed towards the sun and earth rotates under the orbit. The continuous strip images are displayed in 115x115-mile format, and only 30 seconds are required for the satellite to map out this area.

Many LANDSAT pictures are of interest to oceanographers. Figure 5.3 shows the circulation patterns of suspended sediment along the Texas coast, an area of very high erosion.

The mud and silt around the mouth of the Mississippi River in Figure 5.4 illustrates the process of delta building. The Mississippi carries over 1,000,000 tons of silt per day into the Delta.

FIGURE 5.2
Typical Scanning Pattern

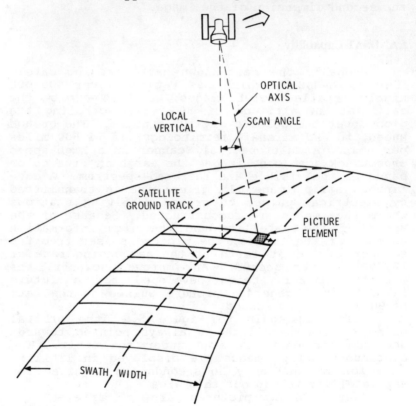

Source: Santa Barbara Research Center

FIGURE 5.3 Suspended Sediment Along Texas Coast

Source: National Aeronautics and Space Administration

FIGURE 5.4 Mississippi Delta

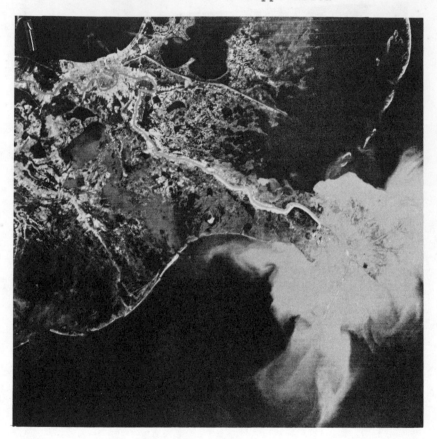

<u>Source</u>: National Aeronautics and Space Administration

Figure 5.5 is a scene off the eastern coast of Newfoundland showing brash ice and drift ice. The effect of the westerly winds is shown in the streamlines on the ice.

The tracking of large ice floes in the Beaufort Sea is shown in Figure 5.6. Successive LANDSAT multispectral scanner pictures mapped the motion over 40 days. Each day's separation of the flow is also shown, and to ice experts the "strain," or distance between floes, indicates that this is a very dynamic movement. These data are fundamental to the development of numerical models for predicting sea ice dynamics. The images of the floes themselves are valuable in understanding the formation, deformation, and weathering of large ice packs. Increased satellite coverage of the northern coast of Alaska and Canada will be needed to support offshore exploration for oil and Arctic shipping through the ice-shear zone.

Now turning to the infrared region of the spectrum, Figure 5.7 shows the temperature patterns in the Gulf Stream as measured at 11 p.m. by an infrared radiometer aboard a weather satellite at 900 miles altitude. This nighttime picture records the self-emitted (black-hot; white-cold) radiation from land, water, and clouds. Figure 5.8 is an interpretive analysis of the infrared view and is important to locating the fast current favored by ships. This current, which is usually about 20 miles east of the west wall of the Gulf Stream, offers a distinct speed advantage over other lanes.

NASA SEASAT Program

In conclusion, let me briefly describe NASA's SEASAT Program. This program will provide a base for the use of space platforms for global and local explorations into the dynamics and resources of the ocean; into the effect of the ocean on weather and climate; and into the role the ocean plays in ice and coastal processes.

Starting with a strong state of knowledge in remote sensing and individual sensor-type demonstrations in other satellite programs, NASA and the Jet Propulsion Laboratory, Pasadena, California, began development of a proof-of-concept spacecraft, SEASAT-A, in 1974. NASA sought the involvement of the agencies and institutions that were the potential users of SEASAT-A data to insure that the needs of these organizations matched the types and

81

FIGURE 5.5
Sea Ice Off Eastern Coast of Newfoundland

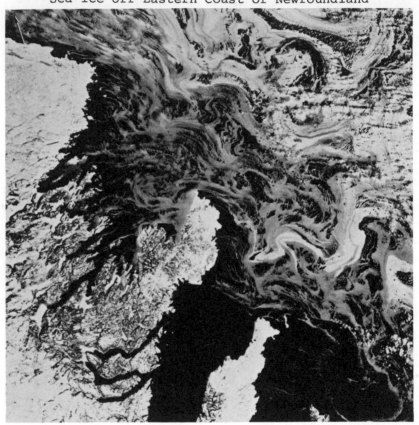

Source: National Aeronautics and Space Administration

FIGURE 5.6 Trajectories of Ice Floes (right center) and
Untethered Buoys (nos. 1 and 6) Tracked by Satellite

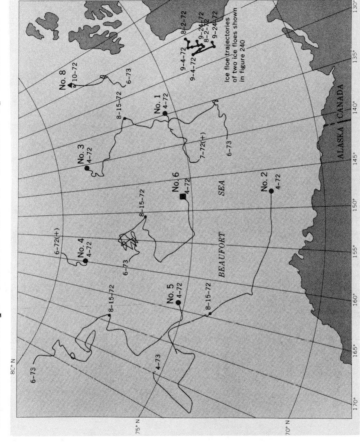

Source: National Aeronautics and Space Administration

83

FIGURE 5.7 NOAA-2 Thermal Infrared (VHRR)

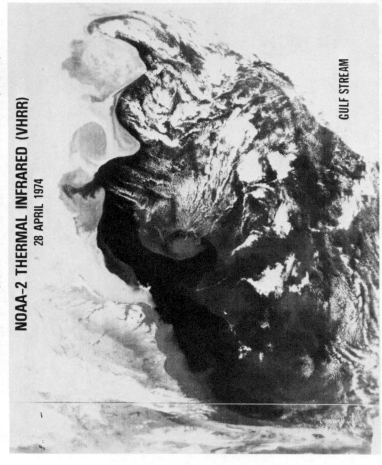

NOAA-2 THERMAL INFRARED (VHRR)
28 APRIL 1974

GULF STREAM

Source: National Oceanic and Atmospheric Administration

FIGURE 5.8
Experimental Gulf Stream Analysis

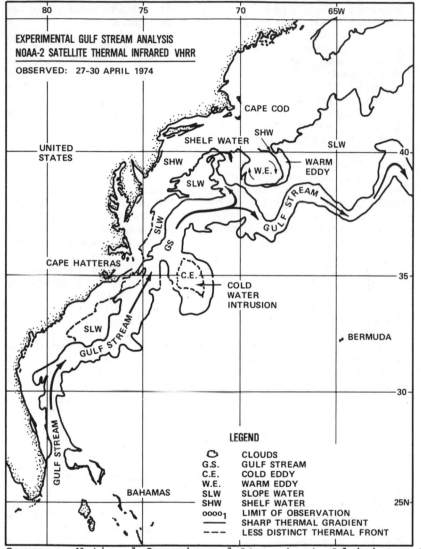

Source: National Oceanic and Atmospheric Administration

quantities of data to flow from the spacecraft and ground processing facilities. From this close collaboration between the "user" community, the mission planners, and the development engineers there evolved a unified "payload" of active and passive optical, microwave, and radar sensors.

A radar altimeter to measure the altitude between spacecraft and ocean surface to ten centimeters and wave heights to fifty centimeters was developed from previously flown designs. Having a precision of ten centimeters will enable the altimeter to see and identify such time-varying features as intense currents, tides, wind pile-up, and storm surges. Wave height data will aid worldwide sea state forecasts.

An imaging radar was developed which can function through clouds and nominal rain to provide wave patterns near shore as well as pictures of ice, oil spills, current boundaries, and similar features. The images will be especially useful for mapping ice leads and open water, and storm wave patterns are important near potential offshore nuclear power plant sites, deep water oil ports, harbors and breakwaters.

A third active radar system is the wind scatterometer which will measure surface wind speed up 10 percent and wind direction to 20 degrees.

A five frequency, passive, microwave radiometer similar to that flown on the Nimbus G environmental monitoring satellite will provide all-weather sea surface temperatues to 1.5°C absolute accuracy. Its measurements of the water vapor in the atmosphere will be used to make corrections to the altimeter and scatterometer measurements.

A visible-infrared passive radiometer will provide reflected sunlight- and infrared-emission images of the oceans and coastal and atmospheric features. It will also provide clear weather surface temperature to an accuracy of 1°C.

The SEASAT-A spacecraft and payload are shown in Figure 5.9. The spacecraft and payload have been built, integrated, and tested preparatory to launch in May 1978 from NASA's Western Test Range at Vandenberg Air Force Base. SEASAT-A will be launched into a 500-mile high circular, polar orbit of 100 minute period resulting in fourteen and one third orbits per day.

The data products of the SEASAT sensors must serve a variety of users in a variety of forms. Weather data is highly perishable and must be processed and disseminated rapidly. Some users care

FIGURE 5.9 SEASAT-A

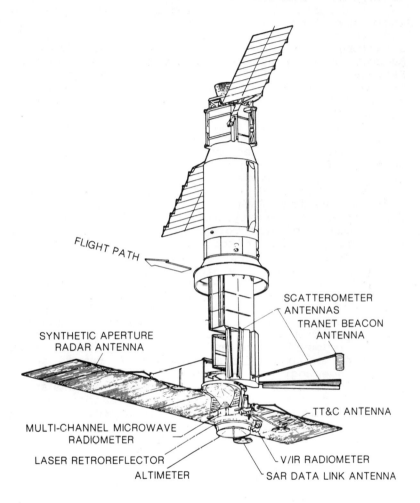

SEASAT—A

Source: National Aeronautics and Space Administration

only for specific outputs such as wind and wave data for ship routing use; others want as much data as available for developing and refining numerical prediction models.

The roster of active users is impressive and includes: Department of Commerce (National Oceanic and Atmospheric Administration, Maritime Administration); Department of Defense (Defense Mapping Agency, Army Corps of Engineers, Navy Weather Service Command, Office of Naval Research, Naval Weapons Laboratory, Naval Research Laboratory, Naval Oceanographic Office); Department of Interior (Geological Survey); Department of Transportation (Coast Guard); Atomic Energy Commission, Environmental Protection Agency; National Science Foundation; National Academy of Sciences; National Academy of Engineering; Smithsonian Astrophysical Observatory; Nationa Center for Atmospheric Research; Woods Hole Oceanographic Institution; Scripps Institute of Oceanography/University of California; University Institute of Oceanography/ City College of New York; and Battelle Institute. From the private sector, the user community includes shipping industry, oil industry, fishing industry, and coastal zone participants.

SEASAT-A is the first major step in developing and demonstrating a global ocean dynamics monitoring system utilizing remote sensing from space. Spaceborne sensors offer a broad range of measurement capability on a spatial coverage scale economically impossible to achieve by any other data gathering method. The application of remote sensing to oceanography not only will provide operational information useful to the maritime industry, but will create better management of the use and misuse of this precious limited resources.

Part III
Political, Economic, and Legal Problems and Opportunities for Using Ocean Space

6

Ocean Enclosures: A Better Way
To Manage Marine Resources

Ross Eckert

The physical quantities of natural resources
that the oceans contain are enormous, but their
economic values to mankind as a whole depends
mainly upon the institutions and ownership arrangements that we establish to control their use. If
resources are extracted too quickly or too slowly,
in ways that drive up production costs and therefore prices, mankind over the long run will be
poorer than would be necessary otherwise. The extent of new wealth that the oceans are capable of
producing--that is, their contribution to the size
of the world's economic "pie"--can be great only if
we successfully design a system of incentives that
rewards both nations and individuals when they
avoid wasteful activities.

As with resources on land, the incentives for
avoiding inefficient ocean uses depends on the
existing structure of resource rights. When property rights are absent, weakly defined, or expensive
to enforce, people find it more rewarding to squan-
der scarce resources. There are differences of
course between resources on land and resources at
sea; some of the latter, especially fish and pollutants, are more expensive to confine to certain
waters. But emphasizing the differences in "fencing" costs for resources of each type can lead to
underestimating their similarities. Analyzing

Ross Eckert, Associate Professor of Economics at
the University of Southern California is the author
of a forthcoming book on the economics of the oceans
and various subjects dealing with regulatory
aspects of the oceans.

their similarities makes it apparent that even relatively simple forms of marine resource ownership,
such as the 200-nautical-mile fisheries or exclusive economic zones, offer potentially dramatic
improvements in avoiding inefficiency. This is
the principal reason for the rise and spread of the
enclosure movement of the oceans. Enclosure is an
economic phenomenon responding to basic changes in
market demands, resources scarcities, and technology. Enclosure is not only inevitable but desirable since it offers a greater prospect for managing marine resources efficiently than any alternative decision-making mechanism.

Ocean Uses in Historical Perspective

Until recent times, the goods and services that
mankind extracted from the oceans were relatively
few and uncomplicated. They provided food and
clothing from fish and animals, buoyancy for shipping and communication, and an area for naval operations to enhance national security. The rule governing the ownership of the oceans for these activities was simplicity itself: there was open access
for any purpose in all areas except for an narrow
band of "territorial seas" adjacent to coastlines.
Ships generally could sail where their captains
pleased and they could establish private property
rights in the fish or other resources that they
found merely by capturing and hauling them onboard.
The number of ocean demands and users was so small
relative to the seemingly endless supply of space
and resources that it made no sense economically to
divide the oceans generally or to restrict access
in many areas (a few choice fishing grounds that
were close to coastlines were the principal excep-
tions).
The nature and extent of ocean activities began
to change rapidly after the close of the Second
World War. Increasing population and technological
change led to greater demands being placed on ocean
space, not only by traditional categories of users
but by entirely new activities that were described
in several of the earlier chapters of this volume.
Briefly, these new categories include: extracting
energy and metals from steadily deeper areas; using
more, larger, and increasingly sophisticated ships
to support a growing volume of international trade;
deliberately dumping or accidentally spilling a
greater variety of wastes and possibly harmful pol-

lutants, with still more materials rafted from land into the oceanic "sink" by weather and by gravity; using coastal areas for multiple recreational purposes; and learning more about the planet's most basic physical and biological processes.

These trends have produced benefits, but they have also caused problems. More shipping has placed greater demands on the use of narrow straits where operations have become increasingly hazardous, especially for supertankers. Certain fishing grounds have become so congested that some stocks are declining. Unlimited competition between incompatible uses also threatens to reduce the wealth that the oceans are capable of producing. For example, offshore oil drilling may cause serious damage to nearby recreational beaches. The disposal of pollutants at sea may reduce fish supplies and create harmful side effects along the food chain. The rising value of petroleum makes larger tankers more economical and gives them incentives to sail close to shores to save on transit time, but the costs of accidents or spills (which are not borne entirely by the tanker operators and owners) can be significant for the local populations. In such cases the results are likely to be economically inefficient: either congestion among similar users is too great or certain activities that society values highly are displaced or even destroyed by incompatible uses that society may value less. Whenever the priority of right is determined strictly by the principle of first-come, first-served -- which is typical of a communal, freedom-of-the-seas regime -- the results can be wasteful.

Communal property rights based on high seas freedoms are economically appropriate only if the bounty of the oceans is virtually limitless relative to the demands, or if demands are static or growing only slowly. But sharp changes in market values and technologies have put this "era of abundance" behind us. It is now clear that scarcity --the basic economic fact of life--applies even to the oceans. As with resources on land, resources at sea usually cannot be extracted without a cost that varies with location and other factors. The greater this cost, the greater the resource scarcity and thus the higher the potential value to mankind as a whole from reducing the economic waste that communal arrangements cause. This in turn requires establishing an economically rational structure of property rights and incentives. For this purpose there are important historical parallels

93

between the conversion of resource rights on land away from inefficient patterns of communal ownership toward relatively private property rights and the movement away from strictly high seas resource freedoms toward the enclosure of ocean resources.

Communal Inefficiencies on Land

Communal ownership arrangements led to inefficient use patterns on land long before those in the oceans.[2] The essence of communal ownership is that no individual has a property right to a resource without capturing or occupying it. The resource in its natural state--such as the bird migrating along a flyway, the fish on its way to spawn, the minerals lying on the bottom of a stream, or unclaimed acres of land--is owned by everyone and therefore is effectively owned by no one. Everyone has a communal right to the resource before it is appropriated, but this communal right has zero value to an individual unless it is converted into a private right by capture or occupation. No one has an incentive or responsibility to make sure that the fish grows to its most valuable size and completes its reproductive cycle before it is caught. In fact, the structure of incentives is quite the opposite: the game that I fail to catch today will probably be captured and kept by some other hunter tomorrow regardless of its size and age, since this is the only way that anyone can establish a private right to it. Since every hunter recognizes that the same incentives apply to his competitors, the rate of appropriation is accelerated to the point where the survival of the species can be at risk. Someone who had private property in the resource stock usually would exploit it at a rate that maximized rather than minimized its value. To give another example, during a land rush people can establish a claim by occupation but not by purchase, with "squatters' rights" during the early California Gold Rush being one of the most famous cases.[3] This process does not threaten the destruction of land as it does for game, but there are still inefficiencies. Resources are wasted in hurrying to the most preferred sites, in excessive congestion, and occasionally in disputes over boundaries and their enforcement.

Communal inefficiencies occur at present in many publicly-owned resources. Streets, parks, lakes and beaches are usually dirtier and more cluttered than their privately-owned counterparts. This applies especially at peak times when demand outstrips the available space (owing usually to trivial or nonexistent fees) and congestion costs become uneconomically high. More freeway collisions occur at the morning and afternoon rush hours. On a sunny weekend people have to get up extra early to get to the public beach in time to find a suitable place to sit, and sometimes there are minor "fender-bender" accidents connected with grabbing a parking place. These costs are high not just because strangers tend to gather in such places but because the ownership arrangements are so weak. Strangers also gather at restaurants and baseball games, but competition here is controlled by the owner of the property who charges a fee for the use of space and in some cases gives preference to patrons who make advance reservations.

The airshed, most streams, and coastal areas are owned communally. Noxious emissions are dumped into the atmosphere because the cost to any individual of reducing auto exhausts to levels that are healthy for society at large exceed the gains that he can capture personally. Factories that dump tainted water into adjacent streams, municipalities that haul sewage and garbage out to sea, tankers that empty their oily ballast near port, and people who rob public (but not private) desert areas of natural vegtation to plant cactus gardens at home are all responding to the perverse economic incentives of the communally-owned resource. Each action is rational for the individual when only his own gains and costs are reckoned, but it is wasteful in its total impact on society and in some cases can result in the premature destruction of resources.

Usually society attempts to reduce the degree of such inefficiencies by setting fines, enacting regulations, or hiring policemen. Some game can be taken only during season with certain types of gear by people who have licenses, and occasionally limits are also placed on the number and size of catches. Fees are charged for some public camping rounds, and traffic laws are designed to curb those drivers who are a bit too aggressive in asserting their communal freeway rights of first-come, first-served. Highways, parks, and beaches often have signs that say "Do not litter" and there are fines for violations (such things of course are unnecessary on privately-owned roads and land). Auto and factory emissions are now regulated to some degree, and licenses may be required before sewage and other materials are dumped at sea. In each instance the rule, fee, or other penalty attempts to reduce the rate of inefficiency in order to approximate very roughly the results that would tend to occur naturally under private ownership. However, the monitoring costs for public facilities are very high and the policemen are rarely available when they are needed most, so many consumers have incentives to break the rules and perpetuate socially wasteful activities.

The greater the inefficiencies, the more rewarding it becomes for society to modify or eliminate communal arrangements. The conversion from communal to relatively private structures of property rights tends to occur at more rapid rates when the market value of resources rises sharply and when new technologies reduce enforcement costs.[4]

One of the clearest episodes in which communal rights were converted to private rights took place on American range land during 1860 to 1880.[5] Before the Civil War, land for cattle raising was plentiful in the midwest and southwest. After 1865, however, populations, the demand for beef, and the number of cattle ranchers increased. Communal land ownership caused inefficiencies of the usual kind, but they were unavoidable owing to the absence of fencing materials. The area had few rocks and there was too little water for lumber or hedgerows. But the invention of barbed wire lowered the cost to ranchers of dividing the communal range into manageable privately owned estates. The value of land and the other resources connected with ranching increased so much that these private parcels were eventually incorporated into the Homestead Act and other laws permitting the leasing of federal lands. The American West then was settled in an economically rational manner.

The conversion of English agricultural lands from communal growing and grazing arrangements to private estates during the eighteenth and nineteenth centuries is perhaps the most famous historical episode of enclosure. This also was essentially an economic response to higher crop values, better transportation, and improved methods of husbandry (one was crop rotation) that made it sensible to reduce agricultural inefficiencies.[6]

Ocean Enclosures to Reduce Inefficiencies

Ocean enclosures have generally followed the pattern of land enclosures. The market value of both the older and the newer ones have increased sharply, and enforcement costs have been reduced by such technological innovations as faster warships, electronic navigational and tracking devices, and satellities--innovations that are analogous to barbed wire in the nineteenth century. The combined trends in market values and technologies have made it practical now to reduce the inefficiencies that strictly open access causes.

The first major enclosure occured in 1945 when the United States claimed the exclusive right to extract the hydrocarbons and other minerals lying on or under the continental shelf adjacent to its coasts and to exploit the salmon fisheries off Alaska. Since then more than three-fourths of the world's 120-odd coastal nations have issued resource claims to minerals, fish, or other resources that usually extend out to 200 nautical miles from shorelines but in some cases a bit farther. As a result, about one-third of the world ocean is now economically enclosed. Almost all such claims are only to the resource contents of the seas; only a half dozen or so actually claim ownership of the ocean itself or the right to restrict navigational as well as resource-extraction activities. As one would expect of economic processes, enclosure has occurred mainly for the coastal areas that are richest in minerals, fish and other resources and for which enforcement costs are lowest owing to the proximity to land.

The incentives of coastal states to avoid inefficient resource uses under a universal 200-mile regime is too complex a subject to be dealt with here.⁷ In most cases, however, enclosure will have positive benefits on efficiency. Its principal economic advantage is to permit the cognizant coastal state to manage resources either by reducing congestion to manageable levels or by making more careful tradeoffs between incompatible uses. For example, if the rate of fishing in some area increases to the point where yields decline or the survival of the species is placed in doubt, enclosure gives the coastal state sufficient authority to limit entry or control catches. If the use of the ocean as a sink threatens its use for other more valuable purposes, enclosure gives the coastal state sufficient authority to assign property rights between the uses or to confine them to different areas. Coastal states will not always reckon economic values accurately and in some cases they may give disproportionate weight to noneconomic criteria favored by certain groups. But the greater the scarcity of the resource or resources involved, the greater the incentives of decision-makers to take economic factors into account. The rising value of ocean resources suggests that coastal states in the future will be better resource managers than their past records indicate if only because the opportunity costs of inefficient management have greatly increased.

The enclosure movement of the oceans not only is preferable on economic grounds to the previous era of freedom-of-the-seas but it is also superior to the treaty under negotiation at the United Nations Conference on the Law of the Sea (UNCLOS). UNCLOS is a twelve year endeavor among more than 150 countries attempting to write a comprehensive treaty that will define the rights and duties of coastal states as they manage resources in their 200-mile zones and will create an international authority to manage the minerals of the deep seabed for the benefit of the United Nations as a whole. But UNCLOS, if it can agree on a treaty, is unlikely to remove many inefficiencies relative to what the enclosure movement can accomplish, and for some resources (particularly vessel source pollution and deep seabed minerals exploitation) it is likely to make matters worse. The reasons for this result are complex,[8] but they boil down the difficulties involved in so many nations attempting to reach a broad agreement on a diverse menu of issues. Beyond these problems, the deliberations at UNCLOS have been laced by ideological differences, power plays, and bickering. The enclosure movement is not quite a perfect means for avoiding all inefficiencies in ocean resource management, but in comparison with the results of UNCLOS enclosure positively shines.

One possible argument against enclosure raised earlier in this volume[9] is that coastal states would use their new authority to monopolize resource use in their zones and to exclude foreign users (principally fishermen) who previously had worked or travelled through these areas withou restraint. But this argument weakens as soon as it is realized that there are both advantages and limits to monopolization. The advantages lie in the reduction in inefficiency that coastal authority can bring. The limits on the revenue that a given coastal state can extract from domestic or foreign users depend upon the availability of alternative supplies. Ecuador, for example, cannot extract a rent from tuna fisheries off its coast that exceeds the price that foreign (mainly Japanese and American) tuna fleets would have to pay to fish in the zones of other countries, just as Egypt cannot extract a fee from ship owners for the privilege of using the Suez Canal that exceeds the cost of sailing around the Cape of Good Hope. Countries that are lucky enough to be situated close to important straits or fisheries can gain through enclosure some amount of wealth relative to the world as a whole (just how much depends upon the particular circumstances and the available alternatives), but everyone benefits at least a little from the better resource allocation that also results. It is often the case with economic processes that decisions made by individuals or countries in their own self-interest have favorable allocational consequences for society at large, and ocean enclosures appear to be no exception.

Conclusions

The enormous physical quantities of resources that the oceans contain will be utilized wastefully unless an economically appropriate structure of resource rights is established. The era of strict freedom-of-the-seas is now almost behind us, largely because it would have caused substantial inefficiencies in the new era of rising demands for ocean resources and changing technologies for controlling their use. The enclosure movement of the oceans--a relatively peaceful and quiet "revolution" in the ownership of marine resources--has come about with very little fanfare but with much potential for reducing economic waste. These relatively "private" structures of resource rights will continue to be adopted, refined, and in some cases extended by coastal states as long as they offer wealth gains that exceed enforcement costs. On efficiency grounds the enclosure movement is preferable not only to strict open access but to the treaty arrangements that UNCLOS is most likely to yield. This puts enclosure in the unambiguous position of being "first best" among all conceivable regimes for governing the future uses of ocean resources. Public policy within the United States and even at the United Nations should avoid any attempt either to erect barriers to further enclosures or to reverse present trends. Enclosures should be welcomed and, if anything, encouraged.

Notes

Some of the materials used in this paper were drawn from Ross D. Eckert, *The Enclosure of Ocean Resources: Economics and the Law of the Sea* (Stanford: Hoover Institution Press, 1979).

1. It is important to keep in mind from the outset the differences between national claims to the ownership of all or certain economic resources in a given coastal area versus the more extreme claim to ownership of the entire body of water and the sea-floor lying under it. Claims of the former kind are now commonplace, whereas the much stronger claims of the latter kind are relatively rare.

2. My discussion is based on Armen A. Alchian and Harold Demsetz, "The Property Rights Paradigm," *Journal of Economic History* 33 (1973): 16-27.

3. A discussion of this episode and of the different property systems that came about during the gold rush can be found in John Umbeck, "A Theory of Contract Choice and the California Gold Rush," *Journal of Law and Economics* 20 (1977):421-37.

4. See Harold Demsetz, "Toward a Theory of Property Rights," *American Economic Review, Papers and Proceedings* 57 (May 1967):347-59.

5. Terry L. Anderson and P. J. Hill, "The Evolution of Property Rights: A Study of the American West," *Journal of Law and Economics* 18 (1975):163-79.

6. The enclosure of English agricultural lands proceeded more slowly than American range land, probably because of the absence of a single overwhelming technical innovation in the English case and the pre-existence in England of a long-standing pattern of communal rights of use.

7. This analysis is presented in Eckert, *op. cit.,* and the conclusions differ somewhat depending upon the fencing costs noted in the text that accompanies note 1 of this chapter.

8. *Ibid.,* chapter 9, and R. H. Coase, "United States Policy Regarding the Law of the Seas," in *Mineral Resources of the Deep Seabed,* U.S. Congress, Senate, Committee on Interior and Insular Affairs, Hearing before the Subcommittee on Minerals, Materials and Fuels, 93d Cong., 2d Sess., pt. 2, March 5, 6, 11, 1974, pp. 1160-1174.

9. See Chapter 2.

7

Protecting the Oceanic Environment

Ruthann Corwin

Successful use of the marine environment for human benefit depends on our recognition of the oceans as systems: as sets of interrelated elements whose conditions change over time. As on land, we can speak of biological elements and their supporting environment as organized into ecosystems, with herbivores and carnivores dependent on the primary productivity of photosynthetic plankton and algae at the base of the food webs (See Chapter 1). Nutrients cycle through the water column, the plants and animals, the sediments, and back again, or are trapped and deposited in deep basins. Sunlight penetrates only to limited depths, but the fundamental energy it provides is carried to deeper dwelling organisms through the movements of animals in the food web and the fall-out from death and decomposition.

Compared to what we know of ecosystems on the land or in fresh water, the marine environment appears far more tolerant of human activities. The vast size of the oceans, and the difficulties of monitoring, have contributed to this view. Our knowledge about changes that may be occurring has been limited by the state of the art of our measuring systems, but in recent decades our ability to detect highly diluted toxins or large-scale current patterns has vastly improved. At the same time, our interest in using the resources of the oceans has grown. The level of activity in

Ruthann Corwin is Assistant Professor of Environmental Planning and Management at the University of California, Los Angeles.

resource production off our coasts has opened "frontier areas" in oil production, has sent us looking for deep-sea nodules, and has put increased pressure on management of biological resources. These activities, the rising use of oceans for transportation of environmentally harmful goods, and the recognition that the oceans are a sink for air as well as water pollution, have called into question the old saying: "the solution to pollution is dilution."

The primary reason that we can no longer rely on the size of the ocean to absorb our wastes, is the recognition through the recent decades of ocean exploration that the ocean is not a single mass of water over a relatively uniform bottom. Rather, it is a set of complicated topographically defined basins and troughs, ridges, and emergent features. These create a variety of habitats for organisms, and catch places for pollutants. The "forests of the sea," the "rivers of the sea," coral reefs, temperate tide pools, floating plankton and their pelagic dependents, tropical estuaries, and other marine and coastal environments mirror the diversity of life-forms and interrelationships found in the terrestrial portion of our biosphere.

Most importantly for the significance of marine pollution to the international debates over the law of the sea, we are beginning to learn how these different marine environments fall within jurisdictional boundaries, and which resources are dependent in some ways on whose national activities. We can classify fisheries by local coastal or migratory habitat patterns, and we can talk about larval dispersion of individual species and the dependence of juvenile forms on different niches. We are also beginning to trace the accumulation of human-introduced materials in the marine environment, and to understand the different ranges of effects, from the regional problems of increased nutrients causing population changes to the more localized pollution problem of a toxic chemical release from a single source.

A disruption in one part of the marine system, whether it is a change in nutrient flow, loss of a species, a change in the physical environment, or introduction of a foreign chemical, can have effects on organisms separate in time and space from the original disruption. The "catastrophic approach" to marine pollution management would be to wait for some disaster to happen, and then search for ways to prevent further damage. The a priori approach is to ask how much can be accommodated as the sources of impact begin to increase, and to set limits, as has been done for radioactive pollution of the oceans.[1]

A natural system at any one time is in a state of dynamic equilibrium in terms of the numbers and roles of its organisms--changes in some elements will bring about readjustments in others to achieve a long-term balance. The essential message of ecology is limitation--there is only so much natural systems can take and only so much they can give.[2] That humans are capable of exceeding these limits has been demonstrated by ancient deserts and recent dustbowls, unproductive rivers and debates over "dead" lakes. Whether these areas will recover naturally over time, or will require massive human effort to restore, they no longer contribute "in productive harmony" to the support of humankind. There must therefore be some limits to pollution directly related to resiliency of a given environment, but the complexities of both any particular environment, and of pollutants and their effects, as discussed further below, make such limits difficult to define.

Under a definition of pollution based on the concept of human use,[3] the adjustments in marine ecosystems brought about by marine pollution can be valued either positively or negatively. Biostimulation--the increase in organisms from the nutrients in sewage wastes--may be seen favorably by those who utilize the fewer, more abundant species benefited, or adversely by those who value diversity of waste-sensitive species which disappear from the affected area.

Where both diversity and abundance decline as the result of pollution, the case would seem more clear, but there are always tradeoffs to be made with other human uses and costs. It is much easier to calculate the value of marine minerals and petroleum, the cost of alternative methods of waste disposal, or the cost of pollution control equipment, and to argue that these outweigh the benefits of preventing pollution in the marine environment. Damage to the abundance of commercial fisheries from pollution can be valued directly but it is difficult to prove. It is even more difficult to calculate the indirect value of noncommercial species as forage for commercial species. Most difficult is placing an economic value on other roles these species play in ecosystem relationships. We have a very hard time setting a value

on diversity, whether in the context of the unique-
ness of a particular area, or in terms of the total
amount of similar ecosystem remaining undisturbed.
The fact that we can measure the value of minerals
today or the current costs of waste disposal, while
it is very difficult for us to estimate the value
of relatively undisturbed marine ecosystems in the
future, has strongly influenced our tradeoff decisions.

The problems of long-term costs vs. short-
term benefits is not unique to marine pollution,
but appears in most environmental problems. In
the case of the ocean, like the atmosphere, the
difficulty of assessing the tradeoffs is seen as
greater because of its nature as a commons. If no
one owns it, there is no incentive to conserve, as
described in Chapters 2 and 6. But as nations extend their claims for use, and as we better understand the local dynamics of ocean regions, the
costs and benefits become more clear. To enter
into the debate over ocean development requires a
general background on marine pollution. The following pages provide an introduction to the types
and effects of pollutants, their distribution and
fate in the environment, research and information
needs, and some thoughts on the social implications of pollution.

Marine Biology and Pollutant Effects

The impact of pollution on marine life is dependent on the characteristics of the individual
organism and its relation to other organisms as
well as upon the type of pollutant itself. A substance may be taken up through the gills, or ingested and then excreted by an organism, or it may
accumulate in a tissue, such as in the brain or in
the fatty tissues of the body. Here, if it is
toxic, it can damage the organism directly or over
time, or it may take part in a process known as
"bioconcentration," which can extend its effects
to other organisms in the food web. Species may
differentially take up both necessary trace elements and contaminants and store them in amounts
higher than in the marine environment. Other animals higher in the food web can then accumulate
contaminants from their food sources as well as
from the surrounding medium. The uptake, reten-
tion, toxicity, and tolerance of pollutants by organisms are governed by many physiological and

environmental factors particular to the individual, including food habits, age, sex, availability of contaminants, temperature, currents, tides, etc.[4]

It is possible for a pollutant to wipe out an entire species of animal without killing even one adult individual. The adverse effect of the chlorinated hydrocarbon DDT (dichloro-diphenyl-trichloroethane) on fish-eating and reptorial birds such as the brown pelican, golden eagle, osprey, Bermuda petrel, and peregrine falcon, is interference with calcium metabolism, preventing adequate eggshell formation (see Figure 7.1), and causing serious population declines in these species. Additional studies have shown reduction of photosynthesis in algae, direct neurophysical effects of compounds related to DDT in other bird species, and harm to fish by reducing their resistance to stress.[5]

Other toxic substances can kill plants and animals outright, especially in sensitive stages of their life cycles, or can interfere with biological processes. For example, some hydrocarbons are similar to organic compounds and can interfere with the chemical signals that shellfish use for mating. The range of possible biological effects is illustrated in Table 7.1 for damage from crude oil and oil fractions. The reader can appreciate the complexity of attempting to predict the impact of an oil spill when realizing that information about all the species present in an area adequate enough to predict the biological effects listed, must be coupled with information about other factors influencing the impact of the oil: natural physical processes affecting the dissemination of oil components in the water column, the physiographic, chemical, and physical parameters of the environment affected, previous exposure of the area to oil and other pollutants, type and amount of oil spilled, season of the year, and weather conditions at the time of the spill.[6]

Types of Pollutants

Not all of the many thousands of different substances that enter the oceans from human activities are likely to produce adverse consequences. Some substances that do are natural to the waters, such as sediment loads, but human activities alter their normal concentrations. Other materials such as DDT or artificial radioactives are foreign to

FIGURE 7.1 Effect of DDT on Bird Eggs

How does DDT affect the reproduction of birds?
An experiment at the University of California
at Davis provided evidence that DDT affects the
strength of the eggshell, causing them to break
in the nest before hatching. Quail were fed a
diet containing different dosages of DDT. Even
low doses produced considerable degeneration of
the eggshell. The photo on the right is a normal,
healthy shell. On the left is the shell of an
egg laid by a quail fed 225 parts per million
DDT for 57 days. The shell is 25 percent thinner,
missing 60 percent of the spongy layer that
gives the shell most of its strength.

Source: (Right, 1150X; left, 1250X Photos taken
by L.Z. McFarland, R.I. Garrett, J.A. Howell,
University of California, Davis. With per-
mission from The Scanning Electron Microscope,
ed. C.P. Gilmore, New York Graphic Society,
1972.)

TABLE 7.1

Potential Damage to Organisms from Pollution
by Crude Oil and Oil Fractions

1. Direct kill of organisms through coating and
    asphyxiation.

2. Direct kill through contact poisoning of
    organisms.

3. Direct kill through exposure to the water-
    distance in space and time from the accident.

4. Destruction of the generally more sensitive
    juvenile forms of organisms.

5. Destruction of the food sources of higher
    species.

6. Incorporation of sublethal amounts of oil and
    oil products into organisms (resulting in
    reduced resistance to infection and other
    stresses--the principal cause of death in
    birds surviving immediate exposure to oil).

7. Incorporation of carcinogenic and potentially
    chemicals into marine organisms.

8. Low-level effects that may interrupt any of
    numerous events (such as prey location, pred-
    ator avoidance, mate location or other sexual
    stimuli, and homing behavior) necessary for
    the propagation of marine species and for the
    survival of those species higher in the marine
    food web.

Source: M. Blumer, "Scientific Aspects of
Oil Spill Problem," Presented at NATO Conference,
Brussels, November 6, 1970, Woods Hole Oceano-
graphic Institute, Woods Hole, Mass. See Note 6.

marine systems. Major categories of pollutants causing concern today are the halogenated hydro-carbons, such as DDT and PCBs (polychlorinated bi-phenyls), heavy metals such as lead, mercury, and cadmium, radioactive substances, petroleum hydro-carbons, and litter, including packaging materials and drums containing chemical wastes. Chlorina-tion and ozonation products from the chemical treatment of water supply and waste water treat-ment are of growing concern. Over 10 million tons of chlorine are used every year in North America to purify water supplies; 3 percent of this amount is estimated to end up in our waterways as organo-chlorines, some of which may be dangerous carcin-ogens.

Thermal discharges, which alter the tempera-ture of coastal areas, and municipal waste dis-charges, with their high organic content (as well as heavy metals, oils, and other pollutants) are also causing alterations in marine ecosystems. Eutrophic, or nutrient-rich, coastal waters caused by an excess of phosphorus and nitrogen in waste waters and land run-off, are giving rise to changes in the coastal ecosystems which are gaining in-creased attention from marine scientists. Micro-organisms in waste sources are an additional marine pollution problem.

It is not surprising that halogenated com-pounds, those with chlorine, fluorine, and their chemical relatives coupled with carbon and hydro-gen, are of concern in the marine environment, since one of their major uses is to destroy un-wanted organisms in agriculture or public health application. DDT is employed against mosquitos in malarial control, and in agriculture, especially in the protection of cotton crops. Hexachloroben-zene is used as a grain fungicide; mirex as a bio-cide against the fire ant. Other uses of halogen-ated compounds are not based upon their toxicity. PCBs are used as dielectrics for transformers and capacitors, in hydraulic and heat-transfer fluids, as plasticizers, lubricating and cutting oils, components of paints and printing inks, sealants, and resin extenders in adhesives. The PCBs used in industry probably consist of at least eight different substances. Since individual chlorobi-phenyls may react differently in the environment and may affect organisms differently, a knowledge of the exact constituents in the starting product and in the environment is needed by scientists to assess their impact on the marine environment. But some individual studies have indicated preferential inhibition of the growth of some species of phytoplankton, mortality of juvenile shrimp, possible involvement in premature pupping of sea lions, and human deaths and morbidity associated with accidental contamination of food by PCBs.[7]

Lead provides an example of human alteration of natural concentrations. The use of lead in paint and in antiknock additives in automotive fuels has introduced lead into the environment in amounts up to an order of magnitude greater than those of natural processes. No direct effects on marine organisms have been demonstrated, but the consumption of lead-contaminated organisms can have serious human health effects. We do not know the effects of long-term exposure to low levels of lead. We know that Americans have the highest average levels of lead in the blood in the world, and that a small portion of our daily intake accumulates in our bones. Under certain conditions, such as feverish illness, cortisone therapy, or in old age, this accumulated lead can be released into the blood at toxic levels. Lead poisioning causes brain damage, convulsions, behavioral disorders, and death.[8]

The chemical forms of an element, which reach the ocean through human activities, may be very different from those which are added by natural processes. The tragic case of neurological damage to fishermen and their families around Minamata Bay in Japan in the 1950s resulted from methyl mercury taken up by the local organisms from mercury wastes discharged by the Chisso Corporation. Microoganisms in the environment can convert non-toxic species of metals to toxic forms as well as performing detoxification reactions. Elements such as mercury, tin, palladium, platinum, gold, and thallium, if converted to methylated forms by microorganisms in the marine environment, could be toxic to higher organisms.

Radioactive substances, from nuclear accidents and power plants, and especially from reprocessing plants and transportation of materials, may also pose serious threats to humans.

Edward Goldberg, in his excellent report to UNESCO, The Health of the Oceans, points out that each local area may have a unique set of pathways that could return radioactive elements, introduce into its waters, back to man's environment. Three types of artificially produced radioactive species are introduced to the oceans by man: (1) the nuclear fuels, such as uranium-235 and plutonium-238; (2) the fission products, arising from the use of nuclear fuels; such as strontium-90 and cesium-137; and (3) the activation products resulting from the interaction of nuclear particles with the components of nuclear reactors and weapons, such as zinc-65 and iron-55. Major artifical radioactives so far detected in the marine environment are listed in Table 7.2. It takes only fractions of a gram of plutonium, the most toxic of these substances, to induce lung cancers if inhaled. Plutonium appears to concentrate in some marine organisms, particularly seaweeds, such as Saragassum. Goldberg has envisioned one scenario for danger through a concentration of plutonium along a coastline from decomposing seaweed washed up on the shore.

We can foresee other problems from pollutants whose use hs not yet accumulated to amounts which are measurable in the marine environment. More than 12,000 toxic industrial chemicals are in use today, and tousands of new chemicals are being registered eary year. Not all of the new ones will be toxic, not all will be widely used, and only some will have properties that can make them dangerous in the environment over time. But very few are tested with any thoroughness, and then primarily for carcinogenicity. In addition, we are only just beginning to understand the dangers of synergistic effects. Two or more pollutants may interact so that their combined effect is worse than any one alone, or two that are harmless separately may be toxic in combination.

For example, elevated water temperature can sometimes increase the sensitivity of some fishes and other aquatic species to the effects of certain heavy metals, pesticides, and other substances. Chlorinated hydrocarbons such as DDT can be concentrated in oil slicks because of their solubility in oil.[11] For every advance we make in the public health, agriculture, industry, and other human endeavors to improve the quality of life, we will have to be increasingly on guard that the unwanted effects of these actions do not in the long run do us more harm than good.

110

TABLE 7.2

Major Recurring Artificially Produced Radioactives
Which Have Been Detected in the Marine Environment

Symbol	Radionuclide	Half life*	
^{90}Y	Yttrium - 90	64.2	hours
^{32}P	Phosphorus - 32	14.3	days
^{51}Cr	Chromium - 51	27.8	days
^{95}N	Niobium - 95	35	days
^{103}Ru	Ruthenium - 103	40	days
^{89}Sr	Strontium - 89	51	days
^{95}Zr	Zirconium - 95	65	days
^{65}Zn	Zinc - 65	245	days
^{110}Ag	Silver - 110	253	days
$^{144}Ce/^{144}Pr$	Cerium - 144, Praseodymium - 144	285	days
^{54}Mn	Manganese - 54	314	days
$^{106}Ru/^{106}Rh$	Ruthenium -106, Rhodium - 106	1.0	year
^{55}Fe	Iron - 55	2.7	years
^{60}Co	Cobalt - 60	5.26	years
^{3}H	Tritium	12.26	years
^{241}Pu	Plutonium -241	13.2	years
^{90}Sr	Strontium - 90	28	years
^{137}Cs	Cesium - 137	30	years
^{241}Am	Americium - 241	458	years
^{14}C	Carbon - 14	5760	years
^{239}Pu	Plutonium - 239	24,400	years

*Half-life is the time when one-half the original radioactive atoms of the element will have decayed - it is a measure of the degree of activity of a radioactive element.

Source: Adapted from Preston, A. "Artificially produced radionuclides which have been detected in the marine environment.[10]

Distribution and Fate of Pollutants

Figure 7.2 shows the National Science Foundation's illustration of the processes that determine the fate of distribution of pollutants in the marine environment.

Under favorable conditions, the pollutants are diluted, dispersed, and transported by turbulent mixing, ocean currents, and migrating organisms. Unfortunately, the oceans are not mixed thoroughly and high concentrations of pollutants exist in local areas. In addition, there are biological, chemical, and physical processes taking place that concentrate pollutants and lead the pollution back to man.[12]

Charles Wurster has pointed out four major factors that make chemicals like DDT a problem: (1) they have broad biological activity that is not restricted to the pest organism; (2) they have great chemical stability, meaning that they do not break down into less harmful substances over time; (3) they are soluble in fatty tissues; and (4) they are surprisingly mobile.[13] This last property is a particularly important point for understanding marine pollution: many substances have a variety of sources and pathways into the environment, and once introduced into a particular location, they do not stay there. Wurster points out eight mechanisms by which DDT can be distributed around the earth, including, despite its low solubility, some in solution in water, but more in suspension, both in water and as fine particles in the air. DDT also absorbs to particulate matter that is washed into the waters, or is picked up by the wind and blown with dust across oceans and continents. We have recently discovered that it can also go into the atmosphere along with water when it passes into the vapor state, a process called codistillation. And lastly, it can be transported in the bodies of living organisms, particularly by migrating birds.[14]

The DDT example illustrates the need to understand the interfaces between the major elements of our environment, the air, water, rocks and soils, and biological organisms, as illustrated in Figure 7.3. The interface processes may be physical, biological, or chemical, as mentioned in Figure 7.2. As we investigate these processes, we are begin-

FIGURE 7.2
The Fate and Distribution of Marine Pollutants

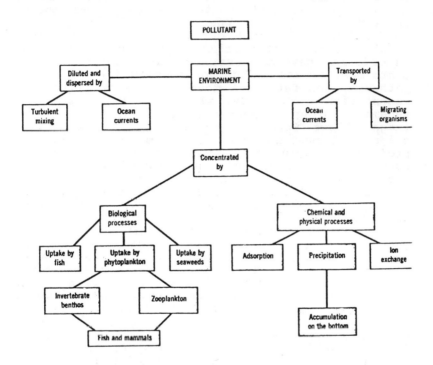

Source: Patterns and Perspectives in Environmental Science, National Science Board, National Science Foundation, 1972

ning to identify the specific mechanisms involved. For example, scientists now classify a variety of mechanisms of the chemical reaction of pollutants in the environment.[15] We must also recognize that when a chemical goes into the environment, it may form derivatives from atmospheric or aquatic reactions, such as in the mercury example mentioned above. Even after long dormant periods, an environmental impact can occur. When an environmental derivative is formed, it then becomes a new chemical with a fate of its own.[16]

In order to make our understanding of these complex interrelationships operational, that is, in order to develop a strategy for control, scientists must create a model of a pollutant's sources, pathways, and fates. A model is a simplified representation of reality, which can be shown by a schematic diagram such as Figure 7.4. Such an image allows workers to visualize the relationships that must be measured in order to make some predictions about the magnitude of possible impacts. In the case of the flow of lead through the Los Angeles area to the coastal waters, J.J. Huntzicker and his co-workers postulated that lead entered coastal waters by at least five routes: dry atmospheric fallout, direct washout from the atmosphere with precipitation, storm-water runoff, river runoff, and municipal sewage discharges. They measured air, soil, and water samples. Based on their assumptions, they calculated the total amount of lead entering the coastal waters as about 5.7 tons a day, from a combustion of neary twenty four tons in automotive fuel. Ten percent of this is estimated to be accumulating in the sediments of the 12,000 square kilometers coastal zone off Los Angeles. About 90 percent therefore either remains in the coastal waters or is eventually introduced into the open oceans.

Sedimentary processes may be thought of as a final sink which removes substances from further use or harm. However, pollutants in recent sediments may be recirculated by the activities of bottom dwellers, and older ones brought to the surface in dredging operations. The U.S. Geological Survey has sampled the sediments of San Francisco Bay, and published a map allowing the U.S. Army Corps of Engineers, which issues dredging permits, to interpret where toxic accumulations might be located. Some coastal sediments can preserve a record of pollution fluxes to the marine environ-

FIGURE 7.3
Pollution Transfer Across Environmental Interface

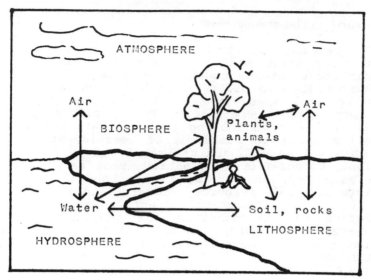

Source: Author

FIGURE 7.4
Flow of Automotive Lead Through the Los Angeles
Area (Numbers are in Tons Per Day)

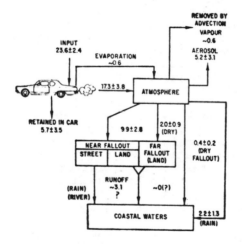

Source: J.J. Huntzicker, et. al, "Material Balance
for Automobile-Emitted Lead in the Los Angeles
Basin," Environmental Science Technology, Vol. 9,
1975. Copyright by the American Chemical Society.

ment, displaying the differences between natural and man-induced processes over time.

Research and Information Needs

Research difficulties abound at every stage of the marine pollution problem. For problems near its coasts, a country can look to its own resources, but in order to look at the world ocean or regional seas, we must have a high degree of international cooperation. This includes cooperation not just in sharing the data gathered, but in collaboration on standards of measurement and experimental methods and ultimately on joint regulation. Corporations and nations must be willing to release data on amounts, timing, and locations of waste disposal, resource recovery, and other activities in the marine environment, to allow for prediction of the magnitude of impacts, possible synergistic effects, and the speed with which action must be taken to head off adverse effects. Such data may be withheld for national security reasons, or because it is held as proprietary data by private interests and governments.

Although concentrations of pollutants are high enough to be of concern, they are still very diluted, and measurements must be made near the limits of sensitivity of the methods of chemical analysis. Results can be biased by the slightest contamination. PCB's, it was discovered, interfered with the detection of DDT, throwing many of the measurements prior to 1966 into doubt. Radioisotopes, on the other hand, are probably the most accurately determined, given the sophistication of equipment which has been developed for measuring these substances over the last thirty years.

We need to know much more about the sinks and reservoirs, the places where pollutants can be stored and accumulated to create future hazards for man, and locations where they may be deposited out of harm's reach. Such latter locations may be difficult to find. We have realized that for shallow waters such as San Francisco Bay, dredging projects mean the possibility of recontaminating the water column. Our current faith in the safety of pollutants in deeper basins further offshore might be shaken by projects such as offshore oil development or deep-sea nodule mining, which have the potential for reintroducing toxic materials into the food web.

116

We need to know more about the rates at which processes occur--how long it takes to decompose a chemical to a harmless substance, or convert it to a toxic one. For each chemical we must describe the entire system of its introduction, movement, and removal from the dynamic environment, and put numbers representing quantities and time periods on the arrow representing each part of the pathways described.

Each pathway must be put in the context of the system of natural and manmade transport paths of materials into the marine environment: rivers, winds, glaciers; domestic and industrial outfalls, and ships. Goldberg has pointed out that the flow of materials from human activity through the environment is approximately 10 percent of the natural material flow.[18] But measurements of the natural rates of transfer of materials are complicated by human activities, such as the increased natural erosion rate from the conversion of forests to agriculture land. Intensive research is required to quantify the pathways even for a simple model.

All this means that the real cost of the good and services that we utilize, and of the disposing of their wastes, must reflect not just by the costs of the damage that pollution might cause, but the costs of understanding these systems for each chemical as well as the direct cost of applying the necessary controls. Marine pollution work requires support services such as sampling stations, vessels, and laboratories. Goldberg points out that there are less than a dozen laboratories in the world capable of measuring DDT or petroleum components in sea water. There are perhaps a similar number of laboratories that are engaged in analysis of radioactive element concentrations in the ocean system. We are in much better shape with regard to knowledge of the more readily measureable heavy metals, which "enjoy an enormous literature."[19] The problems of filtering the significant and consistent information from the variety of diverse samples still make heavy metals an area with many unknowns.

Some of the problems of marine research in a polluted environment are apparent in the efforts of the U.S. Bureau of Land Management to establish environmental "baseline" data from which to assess the effects of their continued leasing of tracts for offshore oil developments. Can we accept the baseline data as time zero? Many scientists have critized the baseline approach as "atheoretical" because it attempts to gather facts without theory. We must start somewhere to measure environmental change over time, but we should do it within the context of the decisions that are being made about uses of the environment. If we use baseline studies for management purposes, there must be a firm commitment from the agencies involved that the studies will continue to be performed in a consistent manner. At the same time, we must recognize that the baseline data could be part of trends affected by natural changes or human activities other than oil and gas development, making any comparisons far less meaningful.

Although it is primarily governmental agencies, and some international ones, who are responsible for monitoring the health of the oceans and interpreting the data, governmental scientists are not well equipped to suggest pollution control strategies, and much effort has taken place outside government circles. There is a serious problem in the translation of scientific knowledge into effective activity. Some private organizations, such as the Cousteau Society, have played major roles, particularly in alerting the public to the dangers. The United Nations Environmental Programme, founded at the 1972 UN Conference on the Environment at Stockholm, is working on the establishment of a Global Environmental Monitoring System, but the level of support and freedom from political constraints remain to be established.

The International Decade of Ocean Exploration (IDOE) took place through the 1970s. Scientists from several institutions collaborated in complex projects managed through systems of steering committees and expert panels. IDOE projects in the Environmental Quality Program have included ocean chemistry, pollutant transfer and effects, baseline studies, and effects of pollutants on plankton ecosystems. The post-IDOE planning report calls for large-scale research, pointing out that research on the oceanography of the continental shelf and slope has involved largely short-term efforts. The report also emphasizes the need for large-scale studies of ocean circulation and mixing on long-time scales, for determination of pollution transport and dispersion. If we are going to store long-lived radioactive wastes in the floor of the deep ocean, we require more biological, geological, and geophysical information, as well as an understanding of ocean mixing over long periods around the globe.[20]

In the United States, the National Oceanic and Atmospheric Administration (NOAA) and the Environmental Protection Agency (EPA) are the two agencies most concerned with marine pollution. Programs such as the Sea Grant College Program support research in the coastal states. Major private and public institutions, such as Woods Hole in Massachusetts, and Scripps Institution of Oceanography in California perform important research along with NOAA and EPA laboratories in different parts of the country. A description of the NOAA, EPA, and Department of Interior relationships, as well as other interesting testimony and background information can be found in the Hearings on Ocean Dumping and Pollution before Congress in 1977 and 1978.[21]

Once an adequate theoretical base for the problems of pollution is established, and rational and effective controls are devised, we will need to develop monitoring systems adequate not only for alerting us to possible dangers, but also for enforcement. The controls themselves are not enough --we must know whether they are being ignored, and we must have international agreements to enforce them. There have been instances where planes have spotted oil being discharged from a tanker but been unable to do anthing about it because the ship steamed into international waters before it could be intercepted.[22] Recent developments such as the techniques of "fingerprinting" spilled oil for identification of offending vessels and emphasis on collision prevention and training[23] may bring some of this pollution under control. Much of the responsibility for marine offenses falls under jurisdiction of the U.S. Coast Guard, whose equipment and manpower must be divided between pollution offense monitoring and its more traditional roles in law enforcement.[24]

Research in monitoring systems required for marine pollution control must combine knowledge of the state of the art in surveillance, control, pollution, and cleanup technology. Technology for monitoring and control may be changing rapidly, in part due to pressures from other sectors in society, such as the satellite monitoring technology described by Robert Hummer elsewhere in this book (Chapter 5), or it may be moving slowly from lack of attention.

For example, despite the increased incidence of marine pollution from oil transport over the last decade, the industry's ability to boom

spilled oil has only extended from spills in two-
to three-foot seas to those in six- to eight-foot
seas. This barely begins to respond to the disper-
sal of oil in rough seas when the damage is most
likely to occur. This form of pollution control
is exceedingly difficult and expensive. Oil companies are not sure they can ever be very effective in preventing dispersion of the oil throughout
the water column, and are reluctant to spend the
money where no short-term damage can be shown.
Such issues lead us back to the social implications of marine pollution, where the tradeoffs between expenditures for research, monitoring, and
control and other social costs must be examined.

Social Implications

The impacts of marine pollution can be described with all the terminology that has arisen
since we codified impact assessment into national
law in 1970 under the National Environmental Policy
Act. We have seen primary and secondary consequences, short-term and long-term effects, local
impacts and those that are widespread or distant,
one-time effects and cumulative impacts. Sources
of pollution may be discrete, such as a single
tanker accident, or continuous, such as municipal
waste discharges. Effects may be directly quantifiable, such as the rise of lead accumulation in
sediments, or indirectly quantifiable, such as the
aesthetic effects of beach litter or oiled sand
measured through loss of income to recreational
communities. There may be physical impacts, as in
the oiling of fishing boats and gear, biological
impacts on marine organisms and ecosystems, and
social impacts on humans, including health effects, economic impacts, and loss of recreational
enjoyment.
We often turn first to economic effects, to
find out what this aspect of human behavior is
costing us and whether it is worth our effort to
spend the money needed for research and control.
The best measures of economic impact are actual
costs in past or present dollars, but unfortunately many marine pollution costs are likely to be
incurred only in the future. There is much debate
today over how to value a future cost or benefit,
and much questioning of the use of discount rates
that represent the lost earnings that would come
to society from the investment of pollution control

money in something else. It takes complex analysis
to predict the value of uncontaminated fish protein
to future generations, and these are always subject
to unforseen variables. It is always appropriate
to ask the scope of concern that is given an ac-
counting in cost/benefit economic studies. As our
knowledge of the pathways of impacts grow clearer,
we are also learning more about possible ways to
take previously unquantifiable impacts into account
--by including values for medical expenses or lost
days of work, alternative research locations, etc.
But these are difficult to assign and always argu-
able --where do you draw the line as to what to
assign to one cause or another in our complex
world?

The role of marine pollution in the calcula-
tion of sustainable yields of marine organisms is
also in question. Overharvesting, rather than pollution, is held to be responsible for the sharp
declines in many species, but populations may remain depressed from a combination of factors including pollution, increased competition from other
species, increased vulnerability to predation, or
other systemic effects. If pollution puts organisms under stress, the cause of actual mortality
may be ascribed to other factors. Large-scale
natural or manmade shifts in the marine environment may throw the steady-state assumptions behind
the concept of sustained yield into doubt. It
would seem prudent for us to play on the safe side,
and count on a low regular yield rather than
attempt to maximize annual take in an uncertain
environment. But the fishing industry and government regulators operate in a political climate that
favors short-term results, while decisions about
ocean development projects may have ramifications
that may overturn short-term projections.

It may seem strange to talk of "sanctuaries"
in a fluid environment, but it is precisely in
those areas where pollution can build up along a
coast that the need exists to establish areas
whose purpose is the preservation of the abundance
and diversity of marine organisms of the locale.
It is only by the study and understanding of what
does exist that we can become aware of what we are
in danger of losing, and the relatively pollution-
free locations will serve as controls for studies
like the cooperative mussel watch, to warn us of
the rise of toxic substances to dangerous levels.

The real danger of the buildup of marine pollution over time, besides the direct hazard to

human life and health, is the loss of individual species, adding to the accelerated decline in biological diversity in the world. Through evolution, information has been stored in the genes of living organisms by the well-known processes of mutation, natural selection, and sexual recombination. Sterling Bunnell has stated this point well:

> The species is the great conserver of biological information, and once lost it will never reappear in course of time. Since it takes somewhere between a few and a million years to produce a new species, with the probably closer to the longer interval, it is evident that the loss of any species reduces the biological information present in our world for the rest of human history...Although perhaps not realized for years, there is, from the moment of extinction, an irreversible loss of possibility.[25]

To those concerned about research and productivity, each loss affects our ability to do science and to maintain stable environments and biologically productive ecosystems. To those with a deep and abiding respect for the beauty and diversity of the world, each loss diminishes the delight we experience in the marine environment and reduces the scope of joy that humanity can have its world in the future.

Notes

1. Edward D. Goldberg, personal communication, April, 1979.

2. William Ophuls, *Ecology and the Politics of Scarcity* (San Francisco: W. M. Freeman and Co., 1977), p. 43.

3. J. Clarence Davies II. *The Politics of Pollution,* (Indianapolis: Bobbs-Merrill, 1970), p. 19.

4. Margaret Merlini, "Heavy-Metal Contamination," Donald Hood, ed. *Impingement of Man on the Oceans,* (New York: John Wiley, 1971), pp. 469-479.

5. Harmon Henkin, Martin Merta, and James Staples, *The Environment, the Establishment, and the Law,* (Boston: Houghton Mifflin, 1971) pp. 54-186.

6. Dale R. Evans, and Stanley D. Rice, "Effects of Oil on Marine Ecosystems: A Review for Administrators and Policy Makers," *Fishery Bulletin,* 72,3 (1974). Blumer (1970) (Table 7.1) cited in the above, p. 630.

7. Edward D. Goldberg, *The Health of the Oceans,* (Paris: UNESCO Press, 1976), pp. 60-64.

8. D. Elwyn, "Childhood Lead Poisoning," *Scientist and Citizen* 10,3 (1968).

9. Goldberg, *op. cit.,* p. 99.

10. A Preston, "Artificial Radioactivity in Freshwater and Estaurine Systems," *Proc. Royal Soc.* (London), Vol. 180B, pp. 421-436.

11. G. Tyler Miller, *Living in the Environment: Concepts, Problems, and Alternatives,* Belmont, Calif: Wadsworth Publishing Co., 1975), p. 289.

12. National Science Board, *Patterns and Perspectives in Environmental Sciences,* U.S. National Science Foundation, Washington, D.C., 1972, p. 245.

13. Henkin, *op. cit.,* p. 29.

14. *Ibid.,* pp. 32-34.

15. Irwin H. Suffett, *Fate of Pollutants in the Air and Water Environments: Chemical and Biological Fate,* (New York: John Wiley & Sons, 1977), p. 2.

16. *Ibid.,* p. 4.

17. Goldberg, *op. cit.,* pp. 42-43.

18. *Ibid.,* p. 29.

19. *Ibid.,* p. 12.

20. National Science Foundation, "Post-IDOE Planning, Report of Workshop on 27-29 June 1977," Washington, D.C.

21. U.S. Congress, "Ocean Dumping and Pollution, *Hearings* before the Subcommittee on Oceanography and the Subcommittee on Fisheries and Wildlife Conservation and the Environment of the Committee on Merchant Marine and Fisheries," House of Representatives, Serial No. 95-42, 1977-78, p. 147.

22. Colin Moorcraft, *Must the Seas Die?* (Boston: Gambit, 1973), pp. 169-170.

23. Larry Booda, "Ship Traffic Control, the Nautical Tower of Babel," *Sea Technology* (March, 1979), pp. 7, 10-16.

24. Donald Taub, Chief, Marine Safety Division, U.S. Coast Guard, Long Beach, Calif., Personal communication, January 23, 1979.

25. Sterling Bunnell, "Pork Barrels and Snail Darters," *Co-Evolution Quarterly* (Fall 1978), pp. 91-92.

8

Management of Marine Mammals

Charles D. Woodhouse

> The whale that wanders round the Pol
> Is not a table fish.
> You cannot bake or boil him whole
> Nor serve him in a dish.
>
> Hillaire Belloc, 1896

One may find it difficult to serve a whale whole, but cut into steaks, it becomes a different matter. For certain cultures marine mammals of all sorts have historically provided an important source of meat, hides for clothing, and oil for fuel. There warm-blooded sea creatures have also served a variety of other purposes. Consider for a moment the uses of live marine mammals.

California sea lions take well to captivity, are intelligent and can be trained. They may be found all over the world in circuses, zoos, and oceanaria. This species is typically captured at an early age and frequently adapts to care and handling within a few days; in a month or so training can begin. As a result, the species is popular among those engaged in the exotic animal trade.

In the last two years authorization was granted by the Commerce Department for the capture of 360 California sea lions. Some will be used for research and some for display. The species

---

Charles Woodhouse is Assistant Director of the Santa Barbara Museum of Natural History and head of its marine mammal programs.

124

does not occur in the Atlantic or Caribbean, but reports of live sea lions from the Gulf and Atlantic coasts are beginning to appear.[2] These are feral sea lions that have escaped capitivity one way or another. No breeding groups have been observed, but there is concern among biologists over the impact on these coastal ecosystems should they proliferate in this new habitat.

Successful attempts by the Navy to train sea lions, porpoises, pilot and killer whales demonstrated that these animals could transport equipment from the sea surface to divers working below, and when outfitted with special harnesses they could locate a dummy torpedo, attach a grapple, and return a lead from the sunken weapon to trainers at the surface.[3]

Uses of marine mammals have, in some cases, led to abuses. Some uses are relatively benign, although we may differ as individuals in our opinions and judgments of capturing wild animals for display. The real abuses have come about in the business of slaughtering or "harvesting" great numbers of these creatures for fur, hides, meat, blubber, and oil. The literature is filled with examples of the decimation of species, where economic extinction has nearly led to biological extinction. Our cleverness with the use of tools has resulted in an increasingly refined technology to take greater numbers with less effort. Paradoxically, we seem unable to rise above the hunter-gatherer level to a more sophisticated, managed fishery before the resource becomes depleted. It frequently seems that it takes some types of governmental regulation to control abuses, but invariably this comes when the species involved is nearly extinct. The regulations are often more concerned with the rate at which the resource may be harvested and less concerned with understanding and knowing the resource so that it can be increased to some level and then harvested, if necessary, under the concept of optimum sustainable population. This trend is gradually being reversed, as reflected in legislation and rules enacted in this country and elsewhere during the last decade.

The International Fur Seal Treaty of 1911 was instrumental in protecting sea otters, even though the treaty itself was concerned primarily with

In the last two years authorization was granted by the Commerce Department for the capture of 360 California sea lions.[1] Some will be used

pinnipeds, and in California, at least, sea otters
were believed to be extinct or nearly so.

Past Conservation Attempts

The protection and conservation of marine mammals typically becomes an international affair.
This is certainly the case for whales. Only with
the establishment of the International Convention
for the Regulation of Whaling in 1946 did serious
attempts to conserve already depleted species get
underway, and even then the organization and resulting treaty were permeated with economic rather
than strictly humanitaritan or environmental moti-
vations. The treaty is a compromise, but it did
establish the International Whaling Commission
(IWC).

This Commission has been criticized by scientists and concerned citizens for many of its resolutions, in particular, those resolutions concerned with catch quotas. The underlying raison
d'etre for these controversial motions stems primarily from Article V of the treaty, which appears
to be at cross-purposes. The Article allows the
Commission to adopt "regulations with respect to
the conservation and utilization of whale resources," while at the same time calls for the Commission to "take into consideration the interests of
the consumers of whale products and the whaling
industry."

The foundation of the IWC was a start at controlling abuses. It has provided an avenue of communication among the member nations and its scientific committee and has been in large part responsible for the evolution of conservation oriented
rather than economic-oriented regulations.

In 1971 a Commerce Department employee who
headed the United States delegation to the IWC that
year stated that the most frequent letter received
in the White House dealt with ending the Viet Nam
conflict. The second most frequent letter dealt
with some aspect of protecting or saving marine
mammals. Congressional hearings that year were
concerned with declaring an international moratorium for ten years on killing all species of
whales.[4] A call for a ten-year moratorium on
whaling was presented by the United States delegation at the IWC meetings in 1972. The concept was
not adopted, but the United States position helped

to make a significant change in the international regulations and catch quotas.

From its inception as a functioning group in 1948 until 1971, the IWC set catch limits in the Antarctic and subsequently elsewhere on the basis of blue whale units (BWUs). This unit of measure was developed in the early 1930s by the principal whaling nations and was probably spawned by economic difficulties from overproduction of oil. An international production agreement was negotiated in 1930 that rated each species of whale according to oil yield in the ratio of 110 barrels per blue whale. For years then the IWC defined and set catch limits as one blue whale unit equals one blue whale equals two fin whales equals two and one-half humpbacks equals six sei whales. The earlier catch quotas were on the order of 14,500 to 16,000 BWUs. These exceeded the ability of the combined whale species to replace themselves and their numbers started to fall rapidly.

At the 1972 IWC meetings, with the United States calling for a ten-year moratorium, it was agreed to abolish the BWU and set catch quotas by numbers of each species. An even more significant step occured in 1974 when it was agreed to set catch limits for each species by ocean area. Blue and humpback whales came under full protection in the 1960s, but at that point, populations of both species were virtually economically extinct.

In 1972 the United States passed the Marine Mammal Protection Act. This legislation carefully regulates the taking or harassment of all marine mammals by United States citizens. There are some pitfalls in this law that have weakened our international position.

The passage of the Marine Mammal Protection Act in 1972 was a significant step toward controlling abuses. It does have a strong conservationist flavor. However, before we call for a total international moratorium on killing all species of whales, it would seem appropriate to get our own house in order. Two major issues are the take of bowhead whales by Alaskan Eskimos, and incidental drowning of porpoises in purse-seine nets used to catch yellowfin tuna.

The native American clause of the Marine Mammal Protection Act allows subsistence hunting of marine mammals by Alaskan natives, that is, Indians, Aleuts and Eskimos. Under this clause Eskimos have been permitted to take bowhead whales even though they are on the United States list of

127

endangered species. As an aside, this legislation caused some consternation among Alaskans because the state constitution makes no distinction between native peoples and other United States citizens.

Under the rules of the IWC there has been a special exemption for aboriginal whaling. The bowhead has been completely protected from commercial whaling since the 1930s. In June 1977 the IWC adopted a moratorium on the killing of bowheads by aboriginal people including native Alaskans. This forced the United States into a rather delicate position relative to our stance on the international level and in our dealing with Alaskan Eskimos.

Bowhead Whale Hunting

If we look briefly at the history of bowhead whale hunting, one can appreciate the concerns behind the IWC resolutions. Bowheads occur in four ranges: the Greenland Sea; in Davis Straight, and Baffin Bay; the Sea of Okhotsk; and finally the area of immediate concern to us, the Bering, Chukchi, Beaufort and East Siberian Seas.[1] In the latter area, bowhead migrate north as the pack ice recedes in spring and migrate south again as pack ice forms extensively in the fall. Principal whaling sites occur at Gambell and Savoonga on St. Lawrence Island and at Kivalina, Point Hope, Wainwright, Barrow, Nuigsut and Barter Island.[5] The whales follow leads in the ice, the narrower the lead the easier a target a whale becomes. Spring hunts generally result in a greater take of bowheads, but other marine mammals are also taken and used in the diet or in other ways. These other species include Beluga, Narwhal and Grey whales, several seal species, polar bear and walrus.[5]

In the period 1928 to 1960 Eskimos at Point Barrow took an average of six bowheads a year, about five in the spring, and one in the fall.[6] But in looking at individual yearly records, the take was sporadic, and in many years none was taken. The most taken in any year for this period was seventeen. One factor that led to present concern over these whales is the increased number of Eskimos who are financially able to purchase whaling gear and thus form hunting crews. A contributing factor is the social status among male Eskimos that is associated with being part of a

successful whale hunt. The greatest status goes
to the captain of a whaling crew.[7,8]

The number of whales struck by harpoons and
lost has grown and is no doubt a result of increased numbers of whalers some of whom are probably inexperienced. The 1975 whaling statistics
show this to be the largest category, that is,
twenty six bowheads struck and lost contrasted to
fifteen killed and retrived and two killed and
lost.[5] If we look at this and compare the figures
for 1976, forty eight were killed and retrieved,
eight killed and lost, and thirty five were struck
and lost.[7] Figures for spring 1977 show: twenty
six killed and retrieved, two killed and lost, and
seventy seven struck and lost.[7] This last set of
figures is disturbing, almost three whales lost
for each one brought ashore.

In September 1977 President Carter was forced
to decide on this problem. In a decision upheld
by Chief Justice Warren Burger, the Carter Administration elected to adhere to the moratorium
adopted by the IWC. Considering our stance on
whaling, there was little choice but to follow the
IWC resolution without severely weakening our international position. Before the December 1977
meeting of the IWC in Tokyo, Alaskan Eskimos
threatened to ignore the one-year moratorium the
following spring. Two issues predominated at the
December meeting. One concerned re-examination of
the 1978 sperm whale quota which was set in the
June 1977 IWC meeting for Japanese and Russian
fleets in the North Pacific. The other concerned
re-examination of the moratorium of Alaskan Eskimos
whaling bowheads. The meeting resulted in, an increased quota for sperm whales from 763 females,
and zero males to 6,444, and removal of the bowhead moratorium to allow Alaskan Eskimos to take
twelve bowhead whales. The two issues are interrelated and at the time of this writing the details
of international bargaining over whaling are not
entirely clear. What appears to have occurred is
that the United States backed off on a strong
stance over the sperm whale quota, and international pressure on Alaskan Eskimos hunting bowheads was reduced, that is, the IWC apparently re-
tracted any attempt to halt aboriginal whaling of
bowheads.

The Eskimos have formed a whaling commission
with the intent of monitoring whale hunts. This
group intends also to initiate changes in hunting
techniques to lower the numbers that are struck

and lost. Heretofore, Alaskan Eskimos have followed traditional whaling methods that are a combination of ancient techniques and those adopted
by nineteenth-century whalers. They hunt from
Umiaks or from the ice edge. Harpoons with explosive charges and bombs fired from shoulder guns
are used, but these weapons are designed after
nineteenth-century models; black powder is used
and the charges are set off by fuses. Compared to
techniques used in commercial whaling, these instruments are primitive and no doubt contribute to
the struck and lost rate.[5,8]

Estimates of the population size of bowheads
vary from 500 to 2,000.[7,8] Some biologists feel
that the population in the Bering, Chukchi and East
Siberian Seas is increasing, but no quantitative
basis has been given. Little is known of their
population dynamics, but as is typical of many
large whales, a cow can give birth every two
years.

If the whale hunt is important to Eskimo culture, then it seems a strictly monitored quota system should be implemented, and the whaling crews
should use modern equipment. On the other hand,
if the whaling crews should use modern equipment.
On the other hand, if the bowheads were fished to
extinction, the Eskimo culture would have to
change as a result. With increased affluence
brought on by development of Alaska's north slope,
bowhead whale products are not vital to Eskimo survival, and there are alternate sources of meat and
blubber. Considering that prior to 1960 many successive years resulted in zero catch, a one-year
moratorium on taking bowheads does not appear to
be a step that would be detrimental to Eskimo culture. The Soviets report that Siberian Eskimos
take bowheads only occasionally.[1] As of December
1977 the question of a moratorium has been dropped,
but it may be worthwhile to consider reinstating
until we have a more complete picture of total numbers and dynamics of the bowhead population. With
proper management of the population, the Eskimos
would fare better in the long term.

Loss of Dolphins and Porpoises

The second major marine mammal problem that I
will discuss is the incidental drowning of porpoises or dolphins in purse-seines used to catch
yellowfin tuna. This problem was nonexistent

before 1960 because the fishing technique involved the use of pole, line and live bait. Tuna fishermen noted that porpoise spotted at the ocean's surface were indicative of tuna below. No one is certain why yellowfin tuna habitually associate with certain species of porpoise, but this realization caused a change in fishing technique. Once porpoises are spotted at the ocean surface, speedboats are launched from the seiner and deployed in order to herd them to an area where the net will be set. Knowing that tuna follow below the porpoises, the latter are circled with a "cup-like" purse-seine net. Once this net is drawn closed at the bottom like a drawstring purse, the porpoise and tuna are trapped beneath.

Fishermen would make efforts to free the trapped porpoise, but the task is not easy and substantial numbers were drowned. Four species are concerned: spotted dolphin, spinner dolphin, common dolphin and stripped dolphin. Different stocks of these species are recognized, and in terms of incidental drowning, mortality is greatest in spotted dolphins and the eastern and whitebelly stocks of spinner dolphins.[9,10]

Protection of these cetaceans is covered in the Marine Mammal Protection Act of 1972, and at the time of enactment, some alarming mortality statistics came to light. Since the Act became law there has been a decline in incidental deaths, but the number still seems high. The mortality estimates of porpoises drowned in tuna purse seines in recent years are: 1971: 312,400; 1972: 306,000; 1973: 175,000; 1974: 99,000; and 1975: 134,000.[11,12]

A two-year waiver on incidental take of marine mammals in commercial fishing operations is contained in the 1972 legislation, but after October 1974 this waiver was over and none could be taken without permit.

In 1976 a 78,000-porpoise quota was imposed on the American tuna fleet. Before the calendar year was out the quota was exceeded and a prohibition on fishing for tuna associated with porpoise went into effect in November 1976. The estimated porpoise kill for 1976 was 104,000.[11]

The 1977 regulations are quite different but still allow a total take of 59,050 porpoises. A major difference in 1977 regulations is establishment of a quota for each of seventeen stocks of porpoises. In addition, fishermen are prohibited from setting on pure or mixed schools of certain

131

species or stocks that are believed to be depleted. These species are the eastern spinner, coastal spotted, and Costa Rica spinner porpoises and melon-headed and pygmy-killer whales.

Prior to the Marine Mammal Protection Act, fishermen experimented with different techniques to reduce porpoise mortality. As a result, two developments held great promise. One is called "backdown." Once a net is set around the porpoises and tuna, the fishing vessel backs down and pulls the top of the purse seine into an elongated oval; the end of the oval farthest from the vessel is pulled underwater and, if timing is right, the porpoises will be concentrated at this point and can swim free. Three to four backdown surges appear to be necessary to spill porpoises from the enclosure. Sometimes crewmen in the water have to pull a few remaining porpoises over the top of the net by hand.[10]

By reducing the mesh of the net in the region where porpoises concentrate during back down, a noticeable reduction in porpoises that drowned by catching their beaks or snouts and their flippers in the netting occurred. This development is known as the Medina panel, and is named after Harold Medina, a tuna boat captain.[10] Refinements included addition of a small mesh apron and Medina panel together form a ramp or chute during backdown that effectively eases the porpoises over the corkline and out of the net. Recent experimental cruises to refine this technique show promise for reducing porpoise mortality; that is, in forty-eight purse-seine nets an estimated 29,000 plus porpoises were caught and then subsequently released. Of these only sixteen were drowned.[13] Thus there seems a positive prognosis.

I think that the creative role of the fishermen should be emphasized, since the notion of backdown and Medina panel came from their quarter; it is the refinements of these ideas that came form the scientific side. The problem is complex, and no doubt the large tuna industry has the strength to lobby for high quotas in the incidental kill of porpoises.

Ideally, I would like to see porpoise mortality reduced to zero. What concerns me is that those animals killed are discarded, presumably because of our stance on whaling. Some carcasses are returned for scientific study, but if we are officially to sanction the take of so many porpoises (e.g., 5,900 in 1977), shouldn't some attempt be made to use this material rather than discard it?

I would like to turn some of these considerations around and look at the effects of total protection.

Progress on Protection

Gray whales were given complete protection in 1947. In California it is perhaps the most familiar whale species and one that can be observed firsthand. The population is now estimated to number 9-15,000. Original stock estimates indicate a size of approximately 17,000. Some aboriginal whaling occurs in the north each year, but the numbers are relatively few, that is, Siberian natives take an average of 160 each year and Alaskan Eskimos about 5 percent.

The gray whale population has recovered remarkably well and has revealed a resiliency that was uncertain in the beginning, but has been demonstrated among other protected species. As the population returns to its original size, it is faced with establishing an equilibrium in an environment that has been altered somewhat because of human encroachment and industry.

Control processes will begin to assert themselves. Top-level predators such as killer whales take their toll, but other factors come into play that are not entirely understood.

During the past several years we have been receiving valid sighting reports of small gray whales in the Santa Barbara Channel at times of the year outside the migration period. In 1977 a number of gray whales appeared dead on beaches here and elsewhere and the number was higher than average. A number of these were shorter than one-year-old animals should be and yet the size pattern of barnacles indicated an age of over one year. One interpretation is that immature whales are not making the full migration to the Bering Sea and back, and some of these may be runts. Thus there may be some evidence that the species is beginning to exceed the carrying capacity of the habitat and "nature" is culling out the weaker ones.

Another phenomenon I believe is being seen around Santa Barbara is that increased numbers relates to an increased probability that some individuals will come into conflict with human activities, for example, entanglement in gill nets and drowning or injury by collision with ships.

In California, sea otters have been protected for a number of years. Sea otters offer a more direct interaction with man than do gray whales. They are under full protection, and as a consequence, their numbers are on the rise and their range is gradually expanding. Since their rediscovery off Bixby Creek in the early 1930s, their range has expanded slightly slower to the north than the south, but today the range includes the coast from Santa Cruz to near Port San Luis. A conservative estimate of their present numbers lies between 1,800 and 1,900 individuals.[14]

Given full protection, the comeback of this species is encouraging, and there is every reason to believe that they will fill out their previous range from Baja California to the Aleutians if unchecked by man or some natural process. There is some question of whether the mammals should continue their range expansion without some form of management. The underlying problem is the conflict between available shellfish for sport and commercial fisheries and sea otters. This is a major issue facing Californians because sea otters simply out-compete man for available shellfish. Within the present sea otter range fisheries for Pismo clam, abalone, and edible crabs are virtually nonexistent. The shellfish concerned are not necessarily in danger of extinction, but the otters take the larger, more easily obtainable individuals, leaving smaller ones behind. The smaller class categories are rarely of value in a fishery. The story of Pismo clams in Monterey Bay will serve to illustrate this point. Sea otters take the larger clams and appear to leave untouched clams of about one-and-a-half to three inches. These small clams are reproductively active so there is no danger of total depletion of clams, but they are smaller than the size limit allowed in the sport fishery.

During the period April 1974 to March 1975 otters began to spread northward into Monterey Bay. The California Department of Fish and Game kept counts of clams during this period and reported approximately 60,000 removed or killed by human activity. A conservative estimate of over 500,000 were removed by sea otters whose numbers in turn averaged from twenty to thirty animals.[15]

The issues related to uses and abuses of marine mammals are complex and frequently involve national as well as international socio-economic considerations. Marine mammals have become a symbol for many environmentalists, but the notion of boycotting Japanese or Russian goods seems a bit simplistic, even hypocritical, when one investigates our own national policies or follows the international bargaining over the harvest of whales. In this chapter I have been able only to summarize some of these issues to make the reader aware of them. I think one of the important unifying threads is the need for effective management of the stocks of marine mammals employing contemporary ecological concepts. Such management is just as important in bringing depleted species to original levels or optimum sustainable populations, as it is in maintaining optimum sustainable populations of species that have increased in numbers since becoming protected. In certain cases marine mammals are inextricably involved with commercial and/or sport fisheries. Under these circumstances the needs of the fisheries as well as the marine mammals have to be considered. In the case of tuna-porpoise, an intensive program in refining fishing procedures to reduce porpoise mortality has produced promising results. In the case of sea otters in California at least, it is a different matter since sea otters are in direct competition with man for certain food items. It then becomes a matter of partitioning the available resource to the benefit of both sea otters and man. Just how this is to be effectively accomplished has yet to be decided and remains a very real challenge in terms of management of both resources.

Notes

1. J. M. Kreps, *Status of Marine Mammals.* Report of the Secretary of Commerce, *Federal Register 42* (147): 38982—39030 (August 1977).

2. Marine Mammal Stranding Workshop, Athens, Georgia, August 10-12, 1977.

3. C. A. Bowers and R. S. Henderson, *Project Deep Ops: Deep Object Recovery with Pilot and Killer Whales,* Naval Undersea Center Technical Report NUC TP 306, 86p. (November 1972).

4. "International moratorium of ten years on the killing of all species of whales." *Hearings* before the Subcommittee on International Organizations and Movements of the Committee on Foreign Affairs, House of Representatives 92nd Congress. H. J. Res. 706 and H. Con. Res. 375 (July 1971).

5. W. M. Marquette, Bowhead Whale Field Studies in Alaska 1975, *Marine Fisheries Review 38* No. 8 (1976), pp. 9-17.

6. W. J. Maher and N. J. Wilamovsky, "Annual Catch of Bowhead Whales by Eskimos at Pt. Barrow, Alaska, 1928-1960," *J. Mammal.* 44 No. 1 (1963), pp. 16-20.

7. J. Walsh, "Moratorium for the Bowhead: Eskimo Whaling on Ice?" *Science 197* (1977), pp. 847-850.

8. S. McVay, "Stalking the Arctic Whale," *American Scientist 61,* no. 1 (1973), pp. 24-37.

9. J. Coe and G. Sousa, "Removing Porpoise from a Tuna Purse Seine," *Marine Fisheries Review,* 34, nos. 1112 (1972) pp. 15-19.

10. E. G. Barham, W. K. Taguchi, and S. B. Reilly, "Porpoise Rescue Methods in the Yellowfin Purse Seine Fishery and the Importance of Medina Panel Mesh Size," *Marine Fisheries Review,* 39, no. 5 (1977), pp. 1-10.

11. D. G. Chapman, Statement presented at *Hearings* before the Committee on Merchant Marine and Fisheries, House of Representatives 95th Congress, first session on reducing porpoise mortality. Serial No. 95-3, p. 228 (May 1977).

12. *Hearings* before the Subcommittee on Fisheries and Wildlife Conservation and the Environment of the Committee on Merchant Marine and Fisheries, House of Representatives 94th Congress, second session on Tuna-Porpoise. Serial No. 94-45; 45-413 (1976).

13. J. M. Coe and P. J. Vergne. "Modified Tuna Purse Seine Net Achieves Record Low Porpoise Kill Rate," *Marine Fisheries Review 39,* no. 6 (1977), pp. 1-4.

14. C. D. Woodhouse, R. K. Cowen, and L. R. Wilcoxon, *A summary of Knowledge of the Sea Otter* Enhydra lutris, L., *in California and an Appraisal of the Completeness of Biological Understanding of the* Species. National Technical Information Service, PB-270 374, 71p. (July 1977).

15. D. J. Miller, J. E. Hardwick, and W. A. Dahlstrom. "Pismo Clams and Sea Otters." California Department of Fish and Game *Marine Resources Technical Report No.* 31, 49p. (1975).

9

Law of the Sea Conference — What Went Wrong

Arvid Pardo

For the past three centuries the law of the sea, which is the legal framework within which man has conducted his activities in ocean space, has been governed by the principle of freedom beyond a narrow belt of sea adjacent to the coast called the territorial sea.

The principle of freedom was based on a number of assumptions. First, that the uses of the sea were limited essentially to navigation and fishing. Second, that navigational uses of the sea were of such a nature as not to require regulation. Third, that the living resources of the sea were so vast as to accommodate virtually unlimited exploitation. Fourth, that man could not seriously impair the quality of the marine environment with his activities.

International acceptance of the principle of freedom of the seas is associated with the ascendancy in international affairs of the maritime nations of Europe, particularly Great Britain, which lived largely by fishing and grew wealthy on trade. Freedom of the seas was in the interest of these nations, and these nations had no hesitation in protecting their interest by the exercise of naval power.

Freedom of the seas began to be eroded with the decline of the traditional naval powers after

Arvid Pardo is Professor of Political Science at the University of Southern California and Senior Scholar at the Institute for Marine and Coastal Studies. Formerly he was Ambassador from Malta to the United Nations, the United States, USSR, and Canada, simultaneously.

the First World War, a decline which was accompanied by radical changes in traditional uses of the sea, by the accelerated development of new uses of the sea, and, in general, by intensification of both new and old uses.

The change in our uses of ocean space have been caused largely by two factors: the accelerated technological revolution which has given us the tools to penetrate, use and exploit ocean space in all its dimensions for an increasing variety of purposes, and the contemporary global population and industrialization explosion which must be sustained by the consumption of enormous and ever-increasing quantities of water, food, raw materials and energy. Increasingly man must turn to ocean space for his needs.

In short, ocean space is acquiring ever-increasing value. At the same time some activities, particularly hydrocarbon and hard mineral exploitation, require the exercise of recognized authority, at least for the protection of investments and of exclusive access to the resource, while a lack of authority beyond national jurisdiction permits depletion of living resources, unnecessary pollution of the marine environment, and, in general, many abuses difficult to tolerate in those areas of the ocean which are intensively used for multiple purposes.

Expansion of activities in the marine environment necessarily involves a corresponding expansion of coastal state interests which, in the absence of an international authority, is normally accompanied by claims to wider areas of jurisdiction and to new rights in the marine environment. This process has been facilitated by the failure of the 1930 Hague Conference and of the 1958 Geneva Conference to reach agreement on precise limits to coastal state jurisdiction in the seas.

By 1967 it had become possible seriously to envisage the possibility of the seabed of the ocean begin divided between coastal states without any serious international discussion. Exploration of the seabed for hydrocarbons was taking place at great distances from the coast, and some companies were beginning to show an interest in the manganese nodules of the abyss. The North Sea had been divided between its riparian states and there was talk of a similar division of the Baltic: some legal experts were beginning to write that the 1948 Continental Shelf Convention had potentially the seabed of all the world's oceans divided between coastal states on the basis of equidistance.

Maltese Proposal

The government of Malta became alarmed at the trend. Malta, in the center of the Mediterranean, is surrounded by the sea. Fragmentation of ocean space under different sovereignties would be certain to obstruct transnational uses of the sea, such as overflight and navigation, vital to Malta's survival. At the same time, a division of ocean space between coastal states would forever confine Malta, which possesses no land resources, to the exploitation of the meagre living and nonliving resources of the Central Mediterranean. Finally, a division of ocean space would inevitably cause tension and perhaps serious conflict. This would run counter to the intersts of Malta, which, as a very small and defenseless state, is vitally interested in the strengthening of international law and order.

It was believed in Malta that division of ocean space between coastal states was ultimately unavoidable on the basis of existing international law, and that hence it was necessary to elaborate a new concept which could replace freedom or sovereignty as the basis of the law of the sea, if developments seriously prejudicial to Malta's interest and to the interests of international order were to be avoided.

It was against this background that the representative of Malta proposed at the United Nations in 1967 that an effective international regime based on the concept of common heritage of mankind be established over the seabed and ocean floor beyond clearly defined national jurisdictional limits, and that an internation organization, other than the United Nations, be created to implement the common heritage concept by administering the seabed and regulating the exploitation of its resources with particular regard to the needs of poor countries. Subsequently the government of Malta suggested that the concept of common heritage be extended also to the sea above the seabed.

The objective of the Maltese proposal was to replace the principle of freedom of the seas by the principle of common heritage of mankind in order to preserve the greater part of ocean space as a commons accessible to the international

139

community. The commons of the high seas, however, would be no longer open to the whims of the users and exploiters; it would be internationally administered. International administration of the commons and the management of its resources for the common good distinguished the principle of common heritage from the traditional principle of the high seas as res communis.

It was hoped by Malta that the establishment of an international organization to manage the common heritage and administer its resources would create pressure to counter the excessive expansion of coastal state jurisdiction in ocean space. Balanced international administration of the greater part of the ocean appeared to promise a number of advantages, including encouragement of closer international cooperation, which could favorably influence events in other fields. Other advantages, it was thought, could be (a) the possibility of creating a framework for the effective management of the living resources of the sea, together with a system of equitable compensation for necessary constraints on the fishing effort of major fishing countries, and for effective control of marine pollution; (b) the possibility of regulating the exploitation of mineral resources in such a way as to ensure significant participation of, and benefit to, poor and geographically disadvantaged countries; (c) the possibility of continuing to ensure maximum freedom of navigation, overflight and scientific research under general international standards, and, finally, the possibility of accommodating foreseeable new uses of the seas, such as mariculture, with other more traditional uses of ocean space.

In any event, the Maltese proposals aroused interest and the United Nations established a committee to examine and report to them.

United Nations Reaction

In the Committee, however, the concept of common heritage aroused considerable controversy, and seemed to be misunderstood even by some professed supporters. The Soviet Union, for instance, said that the concept of common heritage not only did not exist in international law but also that it was impossible to give any clear legal meaning to it. To these objections it was replied that although no area of the globe was presently under a common heritage regime, the creation of such a regime was always possible in international law provided that states agreed on its desirability. As for the precise legal content of a common heritage regime, this was a matter for negotiation within a broad conceptual framework.

On the other hand, it was argued by some supporters of the common heritage concept that any area under a common heritage regime should be administered predominantly, if not exclusively, for the benefit of and by developing countries, with special regard for those developing countries which were exporters of minerals contained in the manganese nodules of the abyss. This interpretation of the common heritage concept was also opposed by Malta, which argued that while due consideration should certainly be given to the needs of developing countries, a common heritage regime should be truly international, and should offer benefits to all countries, whether rich or poor, whether coastal or landlocked.

In the Maltese view the common heritage concept had five basic implications. First, the common heritage of mankind could not be appropriated; it was open to use by the international community but was not owned by the international community. Second, it required a system of management in which all users have a right to share. Third, it implied an active sharing of benefits, not only financial but also benefits derived from shared management and transfer of technology, thus radically transforming the conventional relationships between states and traditional concepts of development aid. Fourth, the concept of common heritage implied reservation for peaceful purposes, insofar as politically achievable, and, fifth, it implied reservation for future generations, and thus had environmental implications.

For Malta the principle of common heritage was conceptually joined with the idea of functional sovereignty, as distinguished from the traditional concept of territorial sovereignty. Functional sovereignty means jurisdiction over determined uses as distinguished from sovereignty over geographic space. Functional sovereignty in conjunction with the common heritage principle would permit flexible inter-weaving of national and international control within the same geographic space and hence secure accommodation of exclusive and inclusive uses of the sea.

By 1970 sufficient agreement had been reached in the United Nations Seabed Committee to permit the U. N. General Assembly to adopt a declaration of principles governing activities on the seabed beyond national jurisdiction embodying most of the suggestions made by Malta. In the same year, also, the General Assembly took the decision to convene a conference which, in addition to drafting an international regime and machinery for the seabed, would also examine all questions related to the law of the sea. The Seabed Committee was reconstituted to prepare the conference.

For a time it appeared that despite continuing opposition on the part of some states, the Maltese proposals would be effectively implemented at least with regard to the seabed, and that serious consideration would be given to reform the agencies of the United Nations system primarily interested in the oceans in order to enable them better to cope with some contemporary problems of ocean space use.

It was during the years 1971 to 1973, for instance, that the functions of the International Maritime Consultative Organization were expanded and that important changes were introduced in the Committee on Fisheries of FAO. It was, however, also during this period that the concept of the patrimonial sea--an area of ocean space extending 200 nautical miles from the coast in which the coastal state exercises sovereign rights over resources--acquired the support of the majority of Latin American States. In 1973 the concept of the patrimonial sea was also adopted by the majority of Asian and African states under the name of exclusive economic zone. At the same time Philippines, Indonesia, Mauritius and Fiji proposed that international recognition be accorded to the idea of archipelagic baselines, an idea which had been rejected at the 1958 Geneva Conference.

Archipelagic baseline, incidentally, means that an archipelagic state may draw straight baselines joining the outermost points of the outermost islands of an archipelago, and that the waters enclosed by these baselines would be under the sovereignty of the archipelagic state subject to the right of transit passage of foreign vessels, and this, of course, if the archipelago is widely dispersed, enormously increases the area under national sovereignty.

142

Law of the Sea Conference

When the conference on the law of the sea con-
vened for its first substantive session in Caracas
in 1974, the situation could be summarized as
follows: First, the majority but by no means all
coastal states supported the concepts of archipelagic baselines and of the exclusive economic
zone; second, there was strong but not majority
support to merging the traditional concept of the
continental shelf with that of the exclusive economic zone, so that the exclusive resource jurisdiction of the coastal state would not extend beyond 200 nautical miles from the relevant baselines; third, there was considerable support, particularly among developing countries, to extending
the principle of common heritage to all ocean
space, both seabed and superjacent waters, beyond
national jurisdiction; fourth, there was general
agreement that an international regime based on
the principle of common heritage should be created
for the seabed beyond national jurisdiction, and
that an appropriate international organization
should be established to administer it in the name
of the international community, but there was sharp
disagreement on the scope and powers of the future
organization and on the manner in which seabed resources should be exploited.

By the end of the Caracas session the general
trend of events which has characterized all subsequent sessions of the Law of the Sea Conference
had become clear. The conference, it appeared,
was more interested in achieving the perceived immediate national goals of coastal states than in
establishing a more viable legal order in ocean
space.

The attempt to extend the common heritage
principle to all ocean space beyond national jurisdiction was decisively defeated at Caracas by the
irremovable opposition of the major maritime
powers, which intimated that they would consider
abandoning the conference if this idea were
pushed. At the same time, implementation of the
common heritage concept with regard to the seabed
beyond national jurisdiction became the occasion
for a bitter debate between developed and developing countries which largely reflected the opposing
points of view expressed at the United Nations in
1974 on the new international economic order.

While the ideals of international cooperation
in the sea on an equitable basis lost ground at

143

Caracas, coastal states, particularly those with long coastlines fronting on the open ocean, demonstrated their control of the conference. All the objectives of these states, exclusive economic zone, archipelagic baselines, imprecise definition of the legal continental shelf, coastal state control over scientific research in national jurisdictional areas, concurrent coastal state enforcement powers with regard to vessel source pollution, etc. eventually obtained the support of the conference majority over th ojections of most landlocked and geographically disadvantaged countries.

Subsequent sessions of the conference have confirmed the ascendancy of the trends established at Caracas, and in the ongoing debate on the functions, powers and methods of exploitation of the minerals in the international seabed area the content of the common heritage concept as proposed by Malta has been gradually lost together with all sense of the realities of seabed exploitation.

Most of the desiderata of coastal states such as archipelagic baselines and the exclusive economic zone have become so entrenched at the conference, that some legal scholars are already arguing that these have become part of international law even though no treaty has yet been signed.

One constructive development which has taken place since Caracas, however, is the development of proposals for a comprehensive system of settlement of disputes relating to ocean space issues.

The latest conference proposals are contained in a document entitled Informal Composite Negotiating Text. These proposals, apart from those concerning the international seabed area, are unlikely to be substantially changed since they are supported by a solid conference majority.

The Composite Text is characterized by emphasis on the political goals of reaching majority agreement on a text, without regard to considerations of equity, to the need for international cooperation in the management of resources and to the need for accommodation of ocean space uses. Controversial issues, such as the delimitation of national jurisdictional areas between states lying adjacent or opposite each other, are dealt with in a vague manner.

The Composite Text proposes that coastal states acquire jurisdiction over marine areas comprising approximately one third of ocean space and containing all known offshore hydrocarbons, 90 percent of the world's fisheries, and a substantial

144

portion of the manganese nodules of the deep sea-bed. These areas, which will come under coastal state control, are also the most important areas of the marine environment for navigation, scientific research, and other uses of the sea. Within these areas coastal states, in addition to sovereign rights over resources, would exercise broad jurisdiction over most ocean space uses with the exception of navigation. Limits of national jurisdiction are imprecisely defined, thus permitting further expansion of coastal states control in the seas.

Beyond national jurisdiction, the traditional concept of the high seas is maintained, while the seabed is proclaimed a common heritage of mankind, but the regime proposed for the international seabed area is simply not viable for a number of reasons. First, the area has no limits, and thus is subject to progressive appropriation by coastal states. Second, the production controls proposed in the Composite Text are such as to make significant production uneconomic when a substantial proportion of manganese nodule deposits are within national jurisdiction. Third, the system of compensation proposed for land-based producers of the minerals contained in the nodules precludes the possibility of significant financial benefits to the international community even in the unlikely event of substantial manganese nodule production in the international area. Fourth, the methods of exploitation proposed are simply unreal. Production is to be undertaken by a massive tax-exempt enterprise governed by diplomats and politicians, and staffed by civil servants, and, on the other hand, by private companies burdened by taxes, royalties and a multitude of obligations. Finally, an authority conceived on the model of the United Nations with multiple commissions and committees is proposed where countries likely to undertake manganese nodule exploitation are not given sufficient voice to prevent decisions harmful to their interests.

Expectations for the Future

So at best, a future treaty based on the Composite Text will legalize continuing appropriation of ocean space by coastal states, and perhaps could have some benefical effect on mineral resource exploitation in national jurisdictional areas, but would serve few other constructive purposes. Such a treaty would not contribute to stability of expectations in the marine environment since many crucial provisions are vaguely formulated, and in at least one-third of ocean space the wide discretionary powers of the coastal states are not even constrained by significant dispute settlement obligations. A treaty based on the Composite Text would not contribute to improved management of living resources, since management of the resources is left to the absolute discretion of coastal states in the exclusive economic zone, and the present freedom of resource exploitation in the high seas remains unchanged. A treaty based on the Composite Text would greatly hamper essential scientific activities in the seas, and perhaps also hamper international navigation. Such a treaty would also contribute to discrediting the idea of international cooperation, since the future seabed authority will simply not be viable. However, most importantly, a future treaty based on the Composite Text will contribute significantly to aggravate world tensions through its fundamental lack of equity. Two-thirds of the area which the Text proposes should pass under national jurisdiction will be appropriated by about two dozen coastal states and archipelagos. Micronesia with a population of 120,000 inhabitants would obtain control of marine areas comparable in size to those obtained by all the other nations of continental Asia with the exception of India. Pitcairn Island with 86 inhabitants would control a marine area more than double the size of that controlled by the Federal Republic of Germany. The United States would double in size and more than double in resources, while a very great number of other states would not only gain nothing but see their possibilities of future access to resources drastically curtailed. I do not believe that an agreement based on a lack of equity will be passively accepted for very long in contemporary political circumstances.

It is difficult to enumerate all the reasons why the law of the sea negotiations, after a promising beginning, have turned into what can only be considered a power play. I attribute great importance to a lack of leadership at the conference in presenting fully, convincingly and insistently the case for new forms of international cooperation in the management and development of ocean space beyond reasonable and clearly defined limits of national jurisdiction. However, lack of leadership

146

can be considered only one of the possible reasons for the unfortunate trend at the conference. Additional reasons which I think have had considerable influence on events include the following: ocean space has acquired a value which it did not have before, and this value is increasing. Governments which have the possibility of expanding in the seas naturally wish to appropriate the greatest possible areas for their benefit since we live in a world of competitive national states, and exclusive access to resources is an element of power which gives states an advantage in their competition with others. This immediate perceived national interest far outweighs in the minds of governments in a favorable geographical position the possible long-term advantages of taking a positive step toward a world based on cooperation rather than competition. This perception is reinforced by the pressure of multiple interest groups within those states.

At the same time it is a fact that states favorably situated for expansion in the marine environment have a long tradition of leadership in all recognized groups at the United Nations and at the conference. The role played at the conference by countries such as Brazil, India, Indonesia, Canada, Australia and Norway in creating a climate of opinion favorable to the immediate interests of their countries has been of very great importance. At the same time negotiations concerning the regime for the international seabed area have suffered not only from lack of intelligent leadership, but have been also bedeviled by an ideological confrontation between developed and developing countries. The negotiations on both sides have become a symbol of commitment to a set of ideological propositions. In the heat of debate the purpose of the discussion and the realities of seabed mining have been lost.

A second major reason for the unfortunate trend of events at the conference has been, I believe, lack of agreement on the purpose of the conference itself. The purpose of the conference, the objectives to be achieved by the conference, have never been discussed officially, but it would appear that for some states the purpose of the conference is purely pragmatic, that is to say, to reach an agreement on a text which can receive the support of two-thirds of the conference participants and which accommodates immediate interests of states. This view of the purpose of the conference results in concentration on the elaboration of formulations which can be variously interpreted and thus receive the support of different groups; but this only postpones problems. Others, however, while conceding the need for formulating proposals supported by a conference majority, believe that the purpose of the conference is to establish a viable and equitable legal order in ocean space which can contribute to creating a new peaceful world order. Views on the nature of such a new legal order, however, vary considerably. The result is total confusion.

This is a rather pessimistic view of the results so far of the Law of the Sea Conference, yet I do not think that it can be yet asserted that the Maltese dream has failed.

There will be a new conference session in Geneva next year, and some states are preparing proposals which, if accepted, will materially improve the Composite Text. Even if these proposals fail, and whatever the final results of the conference, the Maltese dream cannot fail in the long run.

Management of the ocean living resources on a cooperative international basis is becoming increasingly imperative. Scientific research under acceptable conditions is increasingly essential. Equity both at the national and international level is an aspiration that cannot be suppressed. If the world rejects the Maltese dream, therefore, it will destroy itself.

10

Arvid Pardo, the Law of the Sea Conference, and the Future of the Oceans

Robert L. Friedheim

It is fashionable these days to praise or blame Dr. Arvid Pardo, former Ambassador from Malta to the United Nations and now Professor of Political Science at the University of Southern California, for "starting" the train of events which we now call the Third United Nations Conference on the Law of the Sea. The Law of the Sea Conference has now completed its ninth session. It was preceeded by negotiations in an Ad Hoc Committee and then a Permanent Committee. Between the committees and the Conference, the Law of the Sea negotiations are in their twelfth year of periodic meetings. The Conference itself is the largest diplomatic conference ever held (in terms of number of delegates), and most complex (in terms of its number and content of the items under consideration; the draft of a prospective text is 400 to 600 articles long), and if it continues, may be the longest negotiation on record.

It is probably true that the conference output or its consequences will not establish a record as the most controversial or have the most dramatic impact upon the shape of the international system of any conference held. But virtually all observers concede that it has been a very controversy-filled process and that the consequences of the outcome of the Law of the Sea negotiations will have a very substantial impact upon the world system. It will reverse the basic rules by which humankind have used the oceans for the last 370 years. The Conference will ratify, for the most part, a substantial enclosure of ocean space.

We can neither blame nor praise Arvid Pardo for the way in which the delegates of over 150 states have acted in fostering the enclosure of ocean space by their governments. Dr. Pardo, in his 1967 speech, and consistently in a large body of writings since then, tried[1] to point the world in a very different direction. He made his preferences clear in the previous chapter. It is important not merely to note that the world community did not follow his lead, but to ask, why not?

My purpose here is to make a preliminary reconaissance on the question of "why not" so that we all can benefit from the lessons learned in the next major resource-related international negotiation. Arvid Pardo had a dream -- a vision of the future world as it might be. He foresaw a course of action that would lead to what he thought would be a better world. He also had a vision of what course of action the world community could take that would lead to a worse outcome. It appears to him that the world community has chosen the latter. I will discuss the nature of his dreams - both hopes and fears. This should lead us into why Dr. Pardo had this dream; that is, what problems he hoped to solve and where his ideas fit into a long history of western political thought. I will then offer some explanations as to why his dream was not achieved, and will end with a discussion of the consequences of failing to achieve Arvid Pardo's dream of the world adopting what he envisaged as the best course of action.

Concerns of Dr. Pardo

Dr. Pardo's famous 1967 speech reintroduced ocean problems to the United Nations seven years after the First and Second U. N. Law of the Sea Conferences failed to resolve some of the key problems in ocean management. In it, he brought his U.N. colleagues up to date on the developments in human uses of the oceans. Many of these caused him great concern. For one, he feared that rapid development of ocean technologies had caused a jump in ocean exploration activities. If unchecked, he stated, these major new and increased traditional uses of the oceans could upset the oceanic ecosystem. He feared that the ultimate implication of, for example, the unchecked disposal of radioactive waste at sea (quoting Jacques-Yves Cousteau) could be the "closing of the sea to all human uses, including navigation" (underlined in original)[2] Another concern of Dr. Pardo was that in their press to absorb more watery areas as oceanic terri-

150

tory, coastal states, would balkanize the world.
That is, they would act to reduce the rights of
foreigners in their new territory or even exclude
them, thereby making world trade more difficult
and costly and increasing the potential for violent
conflict in the world. He had a third, related,
fear. Improvements in ocean technology opened up
more of ocean space for military uses. Pardo expressed concern that the ability to use the three-
dimensional medium we call sea water and access to
the oceans bottom would fuel the arms race. A
fourth theme woven into his two-and-one-half hour
speech was a fear that in our ignorance of the
nature of the ocean world, our economic exploitative activities in new areas, such as deep-sea mining for manganese nodules, would upset the ecosystem and impinge willy nilly on well established
patterns on land. For example, he was concerned
that whatever benefits mining manganese nodules
could bring to the producers of the metals derived
from nodules, and perhaps to world consumers, such
activities could do enormous harm to the economies
of land mineral producers by driving down prices.
Many land producers of manganese, copper, nickel,
and cobalt (the major consituent elements of so-
called manganese nodules) are developing countries
that depend upon sales of these minerals to provide
hard currency. A price drop could doom their efforts to develop and even perhaps to be self-
supporting.

The fifth concern Dr. Pardo expressed is a
direct out-growth of the fourth. Only major ocean-
using developed states could take advantage of the
freedom to exploit the resources of ocean space.
If the current pattern of ocean economic activity
were unaltered, the gap between developed and developing states would widen even further.

Finally, Dr. Pardo saw the current structure
of international ocean law -the regulatory mech-
anism- as quite inadequate for the regulatory decisions necessary to properly manage the ocean
world. Moreover, change in a limited number of
treaties or judicial decisions would not be adequate to contain the adverse direction of many of
the contemporary trends in ocean use. The regime
or overall framework had to be altered. He suggested that the world community examine the "big
picture" and negotiate an alteration of the regime
that has been used for 370 years-this was Arvid
Pardo's major impact upon contemporary ocean
affairs.

The other side of the coin to Dr. Pardo's perception of what the ocean world was coming to was his vision of what it could become. Dr. Pardo had a hope or dream to match his fears. In addition to perceiving that humankind was abusing its oceanic patrimony, he saw that the world was growing more interdependent and cosmopolitan and therefore it might be possible to alter fundamentally the rules by which the uses of the ocean are managed.

Ambassador Pardo proposed to the United Nations a new regime to manage the seabeds effectively. He soon enlarged it to cover all unmanaged ocean areas and problems. He advocated the division of ocean space into two zones, national and international. In the national area, he would replace the traditional notion of sovereignty with its connotation of total coastal control (which concedes, at most, a right of innocent passage for foreigners) with the idea of jurisdiction of the coastal state. Jurisdiction would allow management by the coastal state but not encourage it to treat the areas under its perview as its exclusive territory.

As long as the outward boundary of the coastal state was reasonably modest, Pardo was less concerned with what nation-states would do within their coastal zones than he was with the fate of the area beyond national jurisdiction. For a majority of ocean space Pardo advocated the elimination of the freedom of the seas concept and its replacement by the notion of the Common Heritage of Mankind. The Common Heritage concept proclaimed that the people of the world would collectively "own" the oceans and that the exploitation of its resources by any and all claimants at their will would cease. This pattern of exploitation by all (communal use) with no control of entry and no principle to control the division of the resource had become extremely destructive. The Common Heritage would allow the assignment of ownership rights to the people of the world and would allow the people's surrogate to limit entry and to establish criteria for how much of the resource could be exploited (with different rules for renewable and non-renewable resources), and for whose benefit. The surrogate Pardo had in mind was a universally based international organization. It would act as the agent of the world's people.

While Dr. Pardo thought and proposed on a grandiose scale, he was responding to a number of specific real world problems. He was also looking squarely at the heart of the general problem. One could argue with Dr. Pardo about the seriousness of each particular problem he raised, and, indeed, I do. But none was a figment of his imagination. More important, I agree that he identified the general problem - the increasing failure of our conceptual framework for managing ocean space. Because freedom of the sea is obsolescent, the decision-makers of the world do not have a firm guideline to help them make ocean decisions that are consistant, and, in the long run, benefical to their own and the world's people.

Theoretical Choices

Conceptually we have only four basic choices (and a large number of "mixes")-freedom of the seas, increasing the common property available to be divided up through appropriate applications of scientific knowledge and technological skill, national enclosure of ocean space, and international enclosure of ocean space.[3] While the first two have valuable elements, they probably are not good guides for a future regime. Retaining freedom of the seas is sensible only if we are wrong in believing that we are destroying the commons by first-come first-served behavior of any user who cares to exploit (open entry). There is too much evidence that Garrett Hardin's "Tragedy of the Commons" is real in regard to the oceans and would continue if we relied upon feedom of the seas as the basis of a future regime. Under a freedom-of-the-seas regime we need voluntary action or willing consent of ocean users (or at least important ocean users) to stop the over-exploitation of the common. We rarely have achieved such consent. Instead, most ocean using states prefer solution that maximize their own short run benefit at the expense of all of our long-run benefits (the "Prisoner's Dilemma").

The second choice, while it is being and should be pursued, alone is not the basis of a viable regime. Human effort deliberately to increase the amount of biological resources of the oceans is limited by presently available knowledge, technology or cost. There simply will not be enough available renewable resources to exploit without changing our habits. If exploitation of larger stocks of renewable and non-renewable resources is attempted under the present regime, the lack of clarity in property right alone could stymie the effort.[4]

This leaves enclosure-national or international. Professor Pardo's preference for central or international enclosure is clear and unequivocal. That is, indeed, what the Common Heritage of Mankind, as he has stated it,is about. Such a centralized approach has all the assets and liabilities of centralizing schemes through the ages. Professor Pardo, steeped in the European tradition of political philosophy, is the worthy inheritor of a series of political thinkers who go back at least to the Stoics.

Professor Pardo, with a Swedish mother (and wife) and Maltese father, has both a Northern and Southern Europe political heritage. I believe both are detectable in his writings. Pardo clearly reflects the influence of Immanuel Kant in his belief that states men should voluntarily enter into agreements that provide for the common good because they will also best provide for the good of the people represented by the statesmen.[5] Statesmen should engage in such acts because they possess "right reason," thus there can be "moral politician(s)". If that is so, leaders and peoples of the world's states should be able voluntarily to chose better collective courses over worse individual courses in their decisions. Only if right reason exists does it make sense for Professor Pardo to propose that states give up their sovereign claims to ocean space in favor of a better common goal, the "Common Heritage of Mankind". The organization Pardo would establish to manage the world's ocean patrimony and end open entry would, if established, fit Kant's criterion of "a Federation of free states."

Also detectable in Pardo's writings is the influence of the poet and (suprisingly to some) political thinker Dante Alighieri. While Arvid Pardo respects the rights of nation-states to exist in harmony- a very Kantian belief-he also has a preference for political institutions that centralize political decisions. Dante developed the fundamental arguments for worldwide political institutions. The following linked quotations from Dante written some 650 years before Pardo proposed a world ocean institution also could serve as justifications for Pardo's proposal:

154

"The knowledge of a single temporal government over mankind is most important and least explored." "Since this theory is a practical science, its first principle is the goal of human civilization which be one and the same for all particular civilizations." "To achieve this state of universal well-being a single world-government is necessary.[6]

I emphasize the intellectual origins of Pardo's proposals because, in concerning ourselves with the future of the oceans, we are dealing with fundamental problems of human political organization. The range of organizational options available has not changed much over time. For the most part only the circumstances under which we must chose one option over the other have changed. Centralizing ocean proposals are heir to both the positive benefits of general centralizing arguments and their liabilities. Pardo, like other centralizers, promises improvements in both efficiency and justice if the world chooses to manage ocean resources centrally. Central notions are comprehensive. No major ocean problem should remain untouched under his scheme. Solutions found to ocean use problems should, if the system works properly, be consistent with each other. Centralization offers the possibility that the linkages of the multiplicity of ocean use issues be understood and efficiently interrelated in terms of solutions. Centralization should reduce costs of management since only one management unit should be able to handle the problems. Justice and efficiency should blend because, under Pardo's scheme, there should be clarity of the collective goals that should be pursued. If proper collective goals are identified, they should be achieved not only because they can be striven for directly but also because there would be a clear recognition of what are primary and secondary goals, and also which are goals that are consistant or inconsistant with the collective goal. Finally, equity and world order would reinforce each other for more practical reasons. Pardo believed that the distribution of the benefit of exploiting resources to the developing countries from the ocean areas belonging to no one would relieve the pressures for redress of past grievences on the Developed by the Developing.

Problems of Centralization

On the other hand, Pardo's ocean centralization scheme must also undergo the usual criticisms of all centralization schemes. These also concentrate on considerations of efficiency and justice. Many will argue that centralization will be inefficient because the complexities of dealing with most ocean use problems in one organization will require a swollen bureaucracy. Others suspicious of centralization will point to "span of control problems" and ask, "is it possible to manage all aspects of human use of 70 percent of the earth's surface in one organization?" Will ocean activities in the world simply prove too numerous and multifaceted to be managed by one organization? Central organizations are known for developing uniform solutions for broad classes of problems. Unfortunately, the ocean world is not geographically and physically uniform. Efficiency and justice considerations require the question--how would a central organization custom tailor solutions to particular problems in many highly varied ocean areas, particularly in coastal waters? Related is the question of assuming that we really know what is in the common good. In a world of imperfect information are we certain we have all the answers we need to make authoritative decisions? Finally, will lack of variety of solutions implied by centralization choke off innovation, and will a single political authority become authoritarian?

These are all questions asked by political philosophers for thousands of years. But they are relevant today as the world's states make fundamental decisions about the future of ocean space. Arvid Pardo has clearly stated his philosophic preferences. Those who oppose Professor Pardo's proposal have been less explicit philosophically. He is out of political power and cannot make authoritative decisions. Many of those who oppose the fundamental direction of Pardo's ideas are in power, and they are choosing to make authoritative decisions that aggregate to their separate states various types of increased control over ocean space.

Alternative Courses of Action

Professor Pardo correctly identified the problem-the abuse of the ocean common. But he

identified only one of the alternate courses of
action open to to the world's decision-makers.
Political leaders, both at the Law of the Sea negotiations and in their home capitals, have decided
to adopt one of the alternate courses open to
them. We will deal later with the question of
whether the alternate solution chosen-national
enclosure-is a true or false solution and whether
the national decision-makers who made the choices
lacked right reason or political morality. The
fact remains that the world is in the midst of a
major enclosure movement. In the late twentieth
century, all major avenues of decision have been
used to move toward expansion of coastal states
rights. States assembled in conference, states
acting unilaterally, and individual human activities have pushed or pulled states further into
the ocean.

It is uncertain whether a treaty will emerge
from the twelve year effort of negotiations in law
of the sea problems. After the ninth session in
the Spring of 1978 the prognosis of a treaty emerg-
ing seem more favorable. Much refining work must
be done, particularly on the question of the fate
of the deep ocean. (This, indeed, will probably
resemble central enclosure, though the form will
not be acceptable to Professor Pardo.) But this
is the exception to the rule. Most of such a
treaty will ratify national enclosures of ocean
space. If signed, such a treaty probably would
include a twelve-mile territorial sea (all states
presently concede at least three). Since there is
no right of innocent air passage over national ter-
ritories, expansion of sovereign zones will probably reduce significantly areas in which free
flight over ocean territory is possible. A Law of
the Sea Treaty would also have 200-mile economic
or fishing zones which would allow coastal states
at least predominant rights to control the resource
uses of those enlarged areas. In many cases these
will be interpreted as national monopoly rights.
In addition, ocean scientists will probably require
the consent of the coastal state to conduct scientific investigations within 200 miles of any
coast. A new legal entity called an archipelago
state would also emerge, which, due to its new status, would have rights to enclose large sections
of waters between its constituent islands. Finally, coastal states, along with the international
community, will have new powers to regulate pollu-
ting practices off their coasts and to acquire new

157

powers to enforce new area-based antipollution regulations (along with the country of the port to
which a ship is heading, often the same as the
coastal state).

But the importance of whether the treaty is
signed in the foreseeable future or not is reduced
by the fact that many of the nationalizing speci-
fications of the treaty are already being enforced
by coastal states around the world. A number of
states, notably the so-called CEP states (Chile,
Ecuador and Peru), have been attempting to enforce
unilaterally a 200-mile sovereign zone or territorial sea since the 1950's. More recently there
have been a spate of 200-mile economic and fishery
zone laws passed by legislatures or promulgated by
executives around the world. Soon the 200-mile
zone will be the rule rather than the exception,
even without a treaty. It is also probably inevitable that not only the area of ocean under
national jurisdiction expand but also the nature
of the rights that coastal states demand. These
rights, many of which were stated in functional
terms (as rights to manage a specific human activity), will probably become more comprehensive in
scope as managers learn to treat the area as a
"system".

Where human beings go, government follows.
Human beings are conducting more of their affairs
in, on, and under the oceans than ever before.
Whether the Law of the Sea Conference adopts a
treaty or member-states ratify it, more management
or regulatory activity will be essential over the
real work human beings conduct in ocean space.
Many of these are major technological achievements,
which in turn require efforts to create follow-on
technology and wise management practices to cope
with the problems caused. We are now capable of
drilling for oil under 1,000 feet of water. But we
must be prepared for possible problems of pollution
and a host of other onshore impacts. Increased frequency of shipments of oil by sea and the growing
size of ships creates the possibility of catastrophic accidents such as the recent grounding of
the Amoco Cadiz. Sea lanes are congested, requiring traffic control rules in places. The growth
in the size of tankers to VLCC class (Very Large
Crude Carriers) has revealed how few ports are
available to berth and unload them and points up
the need to construct deep-water ports offshore.
In the further future is the possibility of constructing offshore nuclear power stations, Off-

shore Thermal Energy Conversation (OTEC) units to extract energy from the oceans, and even possibly the creation of open ocean mariculture farms. Clearly we will need rules to manage them and prevent conflict between incompatible uses.

Reasons for National Enclosure

A discussion of what is happening in ocean enclosure inevitably provides some clues as to why it is happening. But let us summarize the major reasons for national enclosure:

First, nationalism. The "it's mine" syndrome certainly has played an important role in ocean enclosure, especially to the ocean areas immediately beyond traditional limits of national jurisdiction.

Second, coastal states face the immediate impact of changing uses of the oceans. They must find solutions to the real problems, because it is their coasts, their harbors, their environoment that will first feel the impact of a lack of sensible management.

Third, it is easier to state and operationalize the identified self-interest of the specific nation-state than to state the collective interest of all. Most of our previous experience points us in the direction of known and trusted national or subnational management schemes rather than unknown or untested international management schemes.

Fourth, as we discussed earlier, we must face up to the significant theoretical and practical questions we have debated for centuries under the rubric of centralization versus decentralization. Nature has not been uniformly kind to all countries. Will centralization and uniformity promote justice and efficiency? Strong arguments can be marshaled on both sides.

Fifth, the statesmen at the Law of the Sea Conference did not demonstrate that they had right reason. This is not surprising. Nor should we view it primarily a moral failure. After all, the LOS conference is the most complex bargaining environment ever invented by man for the resolution of conflict. With over 150 countries trying to bargain on over 100 major issues under a consensus rule, it is not surprising that many statesmen think they would get decisions sooner if they put the problems that exist physically near their shores under their domestic jurisdiction.

Finally, the North-South Conflict fosters national ocean enclosure. For the South, or poor developing-state group, the Law of the Sea negotiations created an opportunity to push developed states and their multinational corporations with their high-powered exploitative technology further away from their coasts. Schemes which promised Third World countries a better long-run deal through pursuit of a collective good, fell upon deaf ears. They did not want the same thing to happen to "their" ocean resources that they claimed happened to their land resources. They feared that only the developed states with their technology could take advantage of an ocean world in which national boundaries were restricted and the area ruled under "Common Heritage of Mankind" would be maximized. They were unshakable in their belief in increasing national jurisdictions, even though on a comparative basis of square mileage to be acquired, the First (Western) and Second (Soviet) Worlds came out the winners.

What If?

What will be the consequence of the world failing to go in the direction that Arvid Pardo has pointed? It is much too early to have a definitive answer. With little available data, we have only educated guesses to rely upon. My guess is that the consequences of handling many key ocean uses problems on a national rather than international basis will provide a mixed outcome. Under national jurisdiction we will be able to resolve some problems but will handle others less well or not well at all. On balance, I believe we will be able to solve more problems than we fail to solve.

Despite the world not adopting the well-articulated centralization proposal offered by Professor Pardo, we have all benefited by Professor Pardo's effort in stating his vision of a "Common Heritage of Mankind." The world needs philosophers to help us set our goals. Philosophers are necessary in the political process. Arvid Pardo's role in the Law of the Sea debate has been that of a philosopher and fits Immanuel Kant's perception of the role of philosophers in public life:

> That kings should philosophize or philosophers become kings is not to be

expected. Nor is it to be wished, since the possession of power inevitably corrupts the untrammeled judgement of reason. But kings or kinglike peoples which rule themselves under laws of equality should not suffer the class of philosophers to disappear or to be silent, but should let them speak openly. This is indispensible to the enlightenment of the business of government, and, since the class of philosophers is by nature incapable of plotting and lobbying, it is above suspicion of being made up of propagandists.[8]

Arvid Pardo has enlightened the business of creating new laws for the uses of the sea. We all are in his debt.

Notes

1. For a collection of Dr. Pardo's writings, see: *The Common Heritage,* (Valetta: Malta University Press, 1975).

2. Pardo speech, draft copy, pp. 44.

3. See Chapter 2 for a more general discussion of the four regime choices.

4. Committee on Agriculture, Nutrition, and Forestry, United States Senate, *Aquaculture In the United States: Constraints and Opportunities,* 95th Congress, 2nd Session, 1978.

5. The distinction between *should* or *will* enter voluntarily into appropriate agreements should be emphasized. Neither Pardo nor Kant as the following quotation makes clear believed the theory was automatically followed in practice:

> We can scarcely hope to find in the legislator a moral intention sufficient to induce him to commit to the general will the establishment of a legal constitution after he has formed the nation from a horde of savages; therefore, we cannot but expect (in practice) to find in execution wide deviations from this idea (in theory).

Immanuel Kant, *Perpetual Peace* (Indianapolis: Bobbs-Merrill Liberal Arts Press, 1957), p. 36.

6. Dante Alighieri, *On World Government or De Monarchia* (Indianapolis: Bobbs-Merrill, Liberal Arts Press, 1949). pp. 39.

7. See Chapters 2 and 6 for discussions of the pros and cons of national enclosure.

8. Kant, *Perpetual Peace,* p. 34.

11

Problems and Opportunities in Marine Transportation

David L. Glickman

This chapter presents an evaluation of a number of recent developments in ocean transportation, particularly the container ship and the supertanker, which have had an almost revolutionary impact on the patterns and practices of world marine transportation. It discusses briefly the significant role of American enterprise in these developments, and then comments on the impact these two ship types have had on port planning and development, on the labor force on the waterfront, on the structure of the shipping industry, and finally, on U.S. national policy with respect to the Merchant Marine and port planning and development.

Containerization

There are essentially three different types of cargo movements: (1) tanker cargo; (2) bulk dry cargo; and (3) general cargo.

Tanker cargo consists of liquid cargo carried in specially designed tanker vessels. It is the largest single component both in total world trade and U.S. trade, and consists primarily of crude oil and refined products.

Dry bulk cargo consists esentially of coal, phosphates, and other minerals, ores and the grains and other such commodities which move in large volume, frequently as full shipload movements. Bulk

---

David L. Glickman, a consultant on marine transportation, formerly was Advisor for Comprehensive Planning and Transportation Policy of the Port Authority of New York and New Jersey.

dry cargo requires mechanical handling equipment on both land and on vessel for the loading and unloading process.

The remainder, general cargo, is basically cargo which is bundled, crated, cartoned, barreled, or otherwise packaged. These are units which move in relatively small volume by comparison with the bulks. A typical general cargo movement from and to the United States may run from 100 to 500 tons as a single shipment, compared to a tanker full of petroleum or a shipload of grain or coal or the ores which constitute the bulks. Understanding these attributes is essential in order to understand the concept of the container ship.

The most recent data on world seaborne trade suggests that the total volume this year may be approaching the four billion ton mark. About 60 percent of this--about 2.4 billion tons--will consist of tanker movements, largely petroleum movements, but with some smaller volumes of chemicals. The dry cargo bulks will probably account for something on the order of two-thirds of this of the balance, equivalent to about 1.0 to 1.1 billion tons. The remainder, ranging from 500 to 600 million tons each consist of general cargo. This is the smallest share of total world seaborne trade (also of U.S. trade) but in some respects it presents the greatest problems of national policy.

The container-ship is a radically different type of vessel than the typical ship which carries general cargo. In the conventional general cargo ship there may be three or four or possibly five holds through which cargo is loaded and then spread laterally on the interdecks or 'tween decks.

In the container-ship the structure of the vessel is quite different. Visualize for the moment a tic-tac-toe type of structure. The container ship consists of a series of cells which are organized vertically; these cells are proportional to the size of the containers. Handling gear to remove these containers from the vessel is typically on land for the newer generation of vessels rather than on the vessel. This means that in order for a container-ship to be accommodated in a given port, a rather substantial investment must be made by those responsible for port planning and development in gantry crane and other equipment. Cranes alone cost about $3 million per unit.

It also means that unloading can be accomplished more rapidly on a container-ship than a

general cargo carrier. The time cycle for loading/
unloading a container with this equipment may run
from three to five minutes. In terms of productivity, longshore labor can move containers into an
out of a vessel, depending upon the time cycle and
the size of the container (most containers in international trade are standardized on eight by
eight feet, height and width, and twenty-and
forty-foot lengths) at a rate of 500-1,000 tons
per gang hour. This compares with conventional
general cargo handling of approximately fifteen
tons per gang hour as a national average. The
radically improved productivity factors for the
container-ship type of operations suggests why container-ship transportation has become so widely
accepted in international trade, and particularly,
in U.S. foreign trade.

Container shipping, as we know it today, got
its real start in the 1930s when truckers began
hauling containers on trailers, which could then
be detached from the tractor (the mode of power),
enabling the trucker to use the tractor for other
hauling duties while the containers were being
loaded and unloaded at the shipper or receiving
dock. Following World War II, "piggyback" type of
operation which combines truck containers with
railroad movement, went through a period of rapid
growth. It was aided by a U.S. Supreme Court decision in 1954, which resulted in relaxed rules for
such service. The present container-ship concept
in foreign trade developed in the early 1950s from
one truck company's persistence and vision. The
company's management believed that a ship should
be employed in much the same manner as a truck-
tractor-trailer. The company was McLean Trucking.
This pioneering effort in the mid-fifties was instituted by taking some old T-2 tankers and con-
verting them into container-ships for the purpose
of testing the idea. Although the capacity of
these vessels was only 226 containers, these vessels were successful, both operationally and financially. These small container-ships blazed the
trail for the development of present-day container
shipping.

The most recent generation of container ships
carry as many as 1,200 containers. A recent report
by the Maritime Administration showed that there
are currently more than 250 container ships operating within the broad structure of U.S. foreign
trade.

Early planning for container-ship operations was based on the assumption that successful container operations was more likely to develop in U.S. domestic water-borne trade than in foreign trade. There were a number of reasons for this belief.

First, under existing U.S. law, domestic shipping services including coastal, intercoastal, and the offshore services may be provided only by U.S. flag vessels. In foreign trade, shipping services are provided by both American and foreign flag carriers, the latter generally operating at a lower cost. Second, the domestic flag carriers operating in the domestic services are not eligible for either construction or operating differential subsidies. U.S. flag carriers operating in foreign trade are eligible for such subsidies.

Third, there were no customs and regulatory agency controls exercised in the domestic trade which are broadly not applicable to land forms of transportation. Such controls do exist in foreign trade, and present very significant operation and policy problems.

Fourth, in foreign trade, the container-ship operator must meet competition from the conventional carrier, both U.S. and foreign flag. In the domestic trades the container ship operator must also meet the competition of the land-borne modes of transportation, that is, the truck, railroad, and aircraft movement between the different regions of continental United States.

Finally, in foreign trade, container-ship operations are subject to entirely different types of constraints. These include: customs and other regulatory problems and controls; differences in the character and commodity composition of different trade routes; differences in the trucking highway and railroad standard systems and practices abroad; ocean carrier conferences and their practices; labor problems and practices of great variability between nations; national merchant marine policies which also vary sharply among nations; and the technological readiness of many countries (or, if you will, the unreadiness) of many countries to accept this mode of transportation. These constraints initially suggested a relatively slow pace of development of container-ship operations in foreign trade.

What has happened much more quickly than anticipated is that, as shippers and shipping operators evaluated their own specific circumstances and experiences, pressures developed to modify the constraints, nationally as well as internationally. Those responsible for port planning and development began to develop programs to provide suitable physical facilities within the ports. Instead of slow and steady progress, containerization has exploded into an ocean transportation revolution which has already profoundly affected ocean shipping and port planning and development. Depending upon the characteristics of the trade routes, container shipping is already a reality or is in the advanced planning stages. However, containerization has proceded more rapidly among the more economically and industrially advanced nations than those which are still in the early stages of economic development.

Last year, U.S. foreign trade general cargo totalled about 145,000,000 long tons. It is estimated that container movements accounted for about 38-40,000 long tons. It has been increasing progressively year by year.

In New York, which handles the largest volume of general cargo in the nation, about half of the total volume of foreign trade now moves via container ships. The proportions for other ports vary. On the Pacific coast some ports now indicate that container operations account for 30-40 percent of their total volumes of general cargo. The outlook is that both total general cargo and containerized cargo will increase progressively, particularly in the trade between the more industrially advanced nations. The increase will be slower in the case of trade between industrially advanced and the less developed countries. But it is quite likely that within ten, perhaps twenty years, as much as 80-90 percent of total general cargo volumes will be moved by the container form of operation.

There are advantages and disadvantages from containerized operation to different components of the shipping and port industries. From the point of view of the shipping operator, container-ship operations yields several advantages. For example, it has already been suggested that the container-ship operation reduces port costs. The reasons can be derived from statistical indicators that were just presented. The larger container-ships carrying about 1,200 containers. Given a three-to five-minute time cycle container-ships can easily complete their port task of unloading and reloading and move out of port within forty-eight hours. Their "turn-around" time is minimized and labor productivity is maximized.

By contrast, the conventional type of operation has an entirely different frame of reference in terms of both time in port and labor productivity. With a fifteen-ton-per-gang hour average, four gangs working steadily, plus daily crewtime, a vessel carrying 10,000 tons of cargo would, for the loading operation, require ten days in port at 800 tons per day. The container vessel can move the full 10,000 tons of cargo in and out within forty-eight hours. This figures out to forty days in port for unloading and loading a conventional vessel for a complete round-trip, compared with four days in port for the container ship.

About fifty cents of every revenue dollar expended by conventional cargo vessel operators is expended for port purposes. This includes handling of cargo on the vessel, on dock, and in the shed. The reduction in port time therefore has a tremendous impact on the economics of the shipping operator. Reduced turn-around time also produces greater vessel utilization, more round trips over any given period of time, and also has an impact on the size of the fleet. Because of the much greater productivity of the container vessels, a smaller number of such vessels can carry the same volume of cargo as a larger conventional general cargo fleet.

Containerization also a very significant impact on the structure of the Merchant Marine. Because the vessel and its related equipment is so capital-intensive, it has led to a series of mergers, consolidations, and consortiums. In the United States we do not normally allow shipping consortiums. This is more typical of shipping operations overseas. The capital cost of the ships, the containers, and the ancillary equipment is far higher than for the conventional ship. This in turn must be related to the cost structures of conventional-ship operation. Such an analysis suggests that the container-ship form of operation is more economical despite its higher capital cost.

To achieve the maximum benefits of the container-ship form of operation, the cargo should be concentrated at a limited number of ports. This is generally referred to as the "load-center concept." Within the industry there is some disagreement on this, and this disagreement carries over to ports. A conventional cargo ship will typically call at and unload and load cargo at a range

of ports within a given coastal area. This is true
on the West Coast, the East Coast, and Western
Europe, and in fact, in all of the major trade
areas. To maximize the economic viability of
container-ship operation, it is best to concentrate the cargo movements in a limited number of
ports. Ports which are not favored because of this
concept object strenuously to the implementation
of the load center concept. It is a life-and-death
struggle for them because if they do not partici-
pate in the trade, the net result would be for the
port itself to decline. In the United States, the
result is that every major port on the Atlantic,
the Gulf Coast, Pacific Coast, has, over the past
ten years, either already installed container-ship
facilities or is in the process of doing so. And
these are radically different from conventional
cargo facilties. There is the thought in some
quarters, particularly at the national level, that
this has led to some overbuilding of container ship
facilities. Since these are expensive, this in
turn, has led to some suggestions at the national
level for a complete restructuring of the port industry.

What has happened in the port industry is that
there has been a follow-the-leader pattern in planning and development. As one, two, three major
ports began to install and develop container-ship
facilities, other ports, viewing the scene and
realizing that if they were not successful in at-
tracting container-ship movements they would suffer
declines, began to install container-ship facilities. I am not certain there has been actual overbuilding of container-ship facilities. I believe
that over time those facilities which are already
in place, or are now being constructed, will have
the cargo movements to make use of these increased
facilities. Volume will increase progressively as
it has in the past. The real problem is the timing
and the sequence of cargo volume increases and
facility construction.

From the point of view of the shipper, what
benefits does the shipper in foreign trade derive
from containerized shipping? Some benefits have
already been suggested. First, delivery in the
least possible time coupled with reduced port
costs. This is a significant consideration to both
shippers and receivers. Truck waiting time at port
tends to be eliminated or minimized. It is not
unusual in a major port for truck crews to remain
around the port area for six to eight hours a day,

trying to pick up their small lots of conventional cargo. Some ports have therefore instituted specific queueing procedures. This is a cost which has to be absorbed by the consignee or the shipper, depending upon the terms of the trade and pricing arrangements. Second, the container also leads to an improvement in the conditions under which cargo is shipped. There is a reduction in multiple handlers. The conventional cargo movement is actually handled or transferred nine to fifteen times between the time that it leaves the exporter's shipping platform and the time that it is received by the importer. The container system makes it possible to load the container with the merchandise at the shipper's dock or exporter's facility, and not have it opened until it arrived at the importer's platform. This results in a series of benefits. There is less damage. It eliminates many of the problems of stowage aboard ship. The container, rather than the shipment, is the unit of movement. It protects against weather. It protects against contamination by other types of cargo. It should also lead to lower costs in cargo rates and a lower total cost of transportation. If so, both the ship operator and the user of the service benefits.

The impact on labor on the waterfront has already been suggested. But let us examine this problem using as an illustration the situation in the Port of New York. In 1951-52 there were 45,000 longshoremen registered on the bi-state New York-New Jersey waterfront. In 1976 there were 12,000 longshoremen registered. There has been a massive reduction in the number of poeple who earned their livelihood on the waterfront. This has produced a wide variety of social problems. As we learned from the history of the development of our nation, as new industries developed they displaced old industries. The new industries absorbed the labor force. In fact, they also absorbed the annual increment in the labor force. The classic case of this phenomenon is what happened to the buggy makers when the automobile became a dominant force in American society. There used to be approximately 50,000 people engaged in the production of buggies. These workers were absorbed into a mobile industry that today accounts for a great many more jobs, about 2,000,000. Hopefully, those who have been displaced on the waterfront will find other types of employment. But it will take time for adjustment.

169

In the short run, the impact on labor is a very direct one and has produced a demand for what is generally referred to as GAI, the guaranteed annual income concept. On both the East coast and the Gulf coast such a concept is now actually in force, though its implementation varies from port to port. What the notion means is that people who are registered in the longshore labor force are guaranteed an income for a given number of hours whether they work or not. In New York the guarantee is now 2,080 hours a year or 52 hours a week. It varies down the coast: Philadelphia has 1,700 hours, on the Gulf coast about 1,000 hours, and in some places there is no GAI.

In the long run, I would suggest that even in developing nations the container type of cargo handling system will grow and will be used increasingly over time. It will contribute to more effective utilization of resources and to increased international trade.

Containerization and Port Planning

The impact of containerization on port planning and development can best be summarized by noting that the criteria which are used for planning and development of the conventional type of port operation are of no real use in the planning for container-ship facilities. The planning criteria are radically different. In planning for a conventional type of facility approximately four acres of space--two acres of shed space and two acres of backup or upland space--are required for a Class A facility. Such a facility which would have an annual throughput capacity of 90-100,000 tons a year. In planning for container-ship facilities in a port, the requirement for land begins with a minimum of twelve acres and runs to fifty acres. The world's largest operator of container ships, Sea Land Service, now uses a basic standard of fifty acres per berth. The reason for this is that the vans--the containers--take up a substantial amount of space. Depending upon the way the marshaling yard is operated--there are different methods for such operations--the demands can run to as little as twelve or to as much as fifty acres per berth.

In effect this means that a port which does not have much space behind the navigable channel cannot become an effective ship port. This has produced a wide variety of problems in many ports around the world because backup space behind the channel is now at a premium. In New York, for example, this has resulted in a massive shift from the Brooklyn and Manhattan waterfronts to New Jersey. Neither in Brooklyn nor in Manhattan was there sufficient space to accommodate the container form of operation, whereas in New Jersey, on Newark Bay, such space is available.

Another example of differences is in operations that caused differences in planning criteria is the location of cargo handling equipment. In conventional general cargo movement the cargoes are handled with ship's gear, the boom and tackle. In the container ship cargo movement the handling equipment is on land.

There are also differences in the criteria for developing truck and rail facilities. Questions such as how the containers are positioned under the gantry and then moved to their allocated slots in the marshaling yard and positioned there for subsequent movement have created a new breed of port engineers.

New Modes of Marine Transportation and National Policy

Finally, let us turn to containerships, super-tankers, and their impact on national policy. The ports of the United States were originally developed by private enterprise. Public management was first developed in New Orleans, New York, and San Francisco. Today the public agency--the port authority--is responsible for the planning, development, and operation of general cargo facilities. On the other hand, most bulk cargo facilities and tanker facilities are still planned, developed, built, and operated by private enterprise. There is a very significant difference.

The privately owned and operated facilities are often components of larger industrial complexes. The investment in such facilities is factored into final product costs and is treated in much the same manner as is an investment in any other facility. For example, U.S. Steel will build a new mill, or a new ore-handling facility at dockside, and the cost of both will be factored into the final product prices. This is not possible in the development of publicly owned and operated facilities. Moreover, publicly-owned and operated

171

facilities do not have the flexibility to adjust to price changes as quickly as can private enterprise. In addition, they are subject to many more constraints in adjusting their pricing practices. Finally, the basic question of whether the publicly provided facilites should be required to yield a net revenue and not only recoup their cost. In many countries around the world the provision of transportation facilities is regarded as part of the provision of the necessary infrastructure for the development of the economy. This is not the case in the United States, certainly not the case for its ports, which are locally rather than nationally operated.

The advent and growth of the containership type of operation coupled with the growing concern with environmental protection has produced suggestions in recent years for a national master planning approach to port planning and development. The ports of the nation are vehemently opposed to this as a matter of policy. But it should be noted that more than one port authority has publicly opposed such a policy but has nevertheless gone "hat in hand" to Washington to seek subvention of various kinds. The container-ship type of operation focused attention on this issue in a very sharp way. It is an issue which must be resolved in the near future.

I do not know what will ultimately emerge from the present period of transition in port and national relationships. There is a move underway for a substantial change in present federal port policy. In all probability the changes will come about in a fairly evolutionary manner rather than by an all-at-once revolutionary approach. These changes certainly will have a tremendous impact on the future role of the federal government in port planning and development.

Supertankers

Let us turn to supertanker problems. Since the end of World War II there have been four relatively well-defined stages in the development of supertankers. The first stage of supertanker development can be traced to the end of the Second World War. During the war the traditional vessel in ocean tanker trade was developed. It was the T-2 type of tanker with a capacity of about 16,600 deadweight tons or approximately 120,000 barrels

of oil. The second stage consisted of the immediate postwar developments in which the average
size of tankers on order moved up to 25,000-30,000
tons. This period ran until about 1951 when sud-
denly there began a very rapid escalation in the
size of tankers.

The post-1951 history of tanker construction
marked the beginning of the third stage of tanker
development. By the first closing of the Suez
Canal in 1957, tankers on order were already exceeding 100,000 tons whereas in the early 1950s
there was hardly a tanker that exceeded the T-2's
capacity. The order of magnitude of increase was
very striking. These developments were based on
three primary considerations: (1) a sharp and continued increase in world petroleum demand; (2) an
increase in length of haul from sources of supply
to refinery centers and consumption markets;
and, (3) the comparative economics of tanker transportation.

A number of important events occurred during
the third stage that then began with the first
closing of the Suez Canal. This period was marked
by a series of major reappraisals of tanker requirements and dimensions, and the placement of
contracts for new tankers which almost doubled the
capacity of the world tanker fleet. The building
effort also completely reshaped its composition.
There were steady increases in size with the largest tanker in existence in 1956 to a tanker of
270,000 tons which was placed on order in 1965 but
which finally emerged on launching as a 326,000
tonner. This was the first of six vessels constructed by Gulf Oil Company to serve its European
refineries from the Persian Gulf.

The present stage--the fourth stage of supertanker development--really stems from the more
recent events in the Middle East involving the
second closing of the Suez Canal (1967) and the
development of two related concepts. The first is
what is called the transhipment concept, developed
by Gulf Oil, and second, the offshore terminal concept which actually was developed earlier but which
is only now reaching a significant level of discussion and policy determination in the United
States.

Today, supertankers in the 200,000-250,000
ton class are rather common in the oil trade of
the world. The largest tanker now in operation is
of 475,000 tons deadweight capacity and there are

tankers of the order of 1,000,000 tons on the drawing boards.

The economics of tanker development and operation obviously vary from case to case, depending upon the length of haul and other considerations, but there are a number of well-defined principles which have emerged which apply to this field generally. The first is that the total cost of construction, including hull, machinery, outfitting, etc. increases at a slower rate than increases in size and capacity. In effect, the unit cost of construction decreases as size increases, notably up to about the 250,000 ton mark. Above this level the cost curve tends to flatten out. This is a common phenomenon in other forms of facility construction.

Second, the cost of operation, including fuel, crew and insurance, operation and maintenance, and a factor for depreciation, decreases as size increases, and, therefore, also reduces total unit cost.

Third, the large tanker is more economical for long rather than short hauls, and for single rather than mixed product movement. A crude oil carrier operates loaded in only one direction of movement. It returns (deadheads) back empty. The tankers now moving from the Persian Gulf around Africa to the United States or Western Europe typically operate this way, as do most other tankers in world trade that do not carry refined products. It's a one-way movement, and the total cost of operation must necessarily be factored out in terms of the total round-trip cost.

It is important to make a point here with respect to the role of American enterprise. Despite the fact that the major American oil companies played dominant roles in Middle East oil and in tanker operation and utilization, industry sources indicate that until very recently United States tanker trade requirements have had little influence on the actual determination of tanker size and construction standards. The American companies played a dominant role in world oil trade but it was not trade with the United States. Much of what oil the United States imported in the past came from short-haul sources, essentially Venezuela.

Second, there is no major port in the United States which has the capacity to accept supertankers. This is the reason for the present emphasis on offshore terminal construction in the United States. In this context, mention should be made of two elements of national policy. The first is that recently enacted legislation provides that before an offshore terminal may be constructed to handle a supertanker and its cargo, the Secretary of Transportation is required to get the consent of what is called "the adjacent state(s)" before a permit or a franchise may be issued. In effect, this means that the state government in, for example, California could veto any application for construction of an offshore terminal off of its coast. It's a unique kind of provision in national legislation.

The second element of national policy that must be mentioned is the issue of cargo preferences. Less than 2 percent of total U.S. imports of petroleum are carried aboard U.S. flag vessels. With imports running roughly 1,000,000 tons a day, there have been demands that a larger proportion be carried aboard U.S. flag vessels. What was recently proposed was legislation which would have mandated, beginning with 1978, that 4.5 percent of all U.S. petroleum imports be carried aboard U.S. flag vessels. By 1985 the proportion is supposed to increase to 9 percent. That is a lot of tonnage. When the legislation came before the House for a vote, Speaker O'Neil called for a voice vote. On the basis of what he perceived, he ruled the legislation had passed. The normal procedure in a case of this kind, particularly where there is an obvious division in voting, is for someone to call for a roll-call vote. The opponents neglected to do this. It was a parliamentary oversight.

Later, they requested a roll call vote on the cargo preference legislation. Initially, the Speaker ruled that the legislation already had been passed. Opponents then approached the Chairman of the House Merchant Marine and Fisheries Committee and asked him whether he would agree to a review of the vote. He assented, on the assumption that the actual roll call would be in favor of the legislation. However, when the vote finally was taken there was a very substantial majority of <u>nay</u> votes.

This creates some fascinating questions of national policy. The proposed cargo preference legislation has been defeated, at least for this session of Congress. While the issue is now dormant it probably is not dead. It may be reintroduced at any time. We cannot avoid the serious questions which underlie the cargo preference

notion as one of the devices to revive the U.S.
Merchant Marine.

12

Evaluating Management of Coastal Resources

Francis W. Hoole

Regardless of the details of specific policies, their substantive focuses, or the level of
government, there will be common characteristics
among public policies regarding the oceans. These
policies will be the result of highly political
policy-making processes involving numerous policy
makers with varying interests. The policies will
deal with an enormously complex world where information is tentative and incomplete. There will be
complicated tradeoffs involved. There will be no
easy solutions to problems. And, perhaps most importantly, the time is short. We cannot wait much
longer to deal with these public policy concerns.
We need to do the best that we can right now and
subsequently correct the policies and programs as
additional information becomes available.

Among the important questions that we need to
ask about these policies and programs, whatever
they are, will be the following. What difference
do they make? Are the goals being met? Are there
desirable or undesirable side effects? Should a
policy or program be continued or terminated?
Would another strategy actually work better? In
short, what is the actual impact of a policy or
program?

This year, some of us in the social sciences
at the Institute for Marine and Coastal Studies at
the University of Southern California have under-

Francis W. Hoole, an expert on evaluation research,
is Associate Professor of Political Science at
Indiana University. During 1977 he was a resident
scholar at the Institute for Marine and Coastal
Studies, University of Southern California.

taken the task of examining how the impact of marine and coastal policies can be determined, and we have been focusing recently on the utility of the evaluation research approach. I would like to share some of my tentative thoughts on this subject with you. I will discuss the evaluation research movement, the evaluation research approach, and the potential uses of evaluation research in the marine and coastal field. Finally, I would like to share some tentative conclusions with you. I must warn you, however, that I do not have all of the answers to questions about the uses, advantages, and limitations associated with the use of the evaluation research approach in the marine and coastal field. I still have a great deal to learn about this complicated and fascinating subject.

Growing Interest in Evaluation

In recent years there has been a growing interest in the use of systematic techniques for the evaluation of the impact of social action programs. This has led to a widespread use of social science methodology in the evaluation of policies and programs in the public sector and to the development of a cross-disciplinary evaluation research movement. Among those involved in the movement are political scientists, sociologists, educators, psychologists, doctors, economists, anthropologists, lawyers, statisticians, and operations researchers, as well as legislators and bureaucrats. In some ways the evaluation research movement can be seen as part of the fallout from the War on Poverty and as resulting from its emphasis on changing societal conditions through social action programs.

What are the indicators of the current interest in the evaluation research movement? There have been over 150 social experiments and numerous non-experimental studies that have been undertaken to evaluate the impact of social action programs.[1] There are two new journals, Evaluation and Evaluation Quarterly, and a new yearbook, Evaluation Studies Review Annual,[2] which are devoted to publishing papers on evaluation research subjects. A Handbook of Evaluation Research was published recently.[3] The National Science Foundation and the Social Science Research Council have recently emphasized the need for evaluation research studies. There is a growing number of governmental

178

jobs in evaluation research. Classes are now being offered on the subject of evaluation research
at numerous American universities. And, in 1976,
an Evaluation Research Society was founded.

Furthermore, practitioners in various types
of governmental agencies have demonstrated an interest in learning more about evaluation research.
For example, high-level U.S. federal government
bureaucrats attended the evaluation research
panels at the 1976 American Society for Public Administration meetings and the Swedish National
Audit Bureau recently initiated a program on effectiveness auditing,[4] which is a variation on the
evaluation research theme. Most importantly, for
our purposes, members of the Institute for Marine
and Coastal Studies at the University of Southern
California have recently discovered an interest in
exploring the possibilities of the evaluation research approach on the part of governmental officials working on coastal zone problems.

Evaluation Research Approach

What is the approach utilized by this movement? Most evaluation researchers probably would
agree with Joseph S. Wholey and his associates when
they contend that "evaluation research is the application of the scientific method to experience
with public programs to learn what happens as a
result of program activities."[5]

The evaluation research approach is concerned
with the full range of operational procedures involved in the systematic empirical examination of
hypotheses regarding the impact of social action
programs. Thus it utilizes a hypothesis testing
orientation, where the hypothesis involves conjec-
ture regarding the impact of a social action program. The evaluation research approach follows a
falsification strategy in testing impact hypotheses. Correlation is not confused with causation
and a systematic effort to disconfirm the obtained
results is required through the examination of
plausible rival explanations. The work of psychologist Donald T. Campbell and his associates provides the basic methodological orientation for the
evaluation research approach.[6] Campbell and his
associates have presented approximately twenty
different experimental, quasi-experimental, and
pre-experimental designs that are useful in various circumstances for controlling plausible rival

179

hypotheses and evaluating the impact of public policies.

I will not present here the details of the methodology of evaluation research. Essentially, the evaluation research approach asks questions about what impacts public policies actually are having, and requires that evidence regarding those impacts be stated in non-equivocal scientific terms. The main concern of evaluation research is obtaining sound empirical evidence regarding the effectiveness of social action programs. The evidence can be used as the basis for optimization, cost benefit and other analyses, or simply as general information for policy makers, those to whom policy makers are responsible, and scholars.

As a political scientist, my concerns start where the work of the ocean scientists and engineers stop. Even when it is possible to develop scientific and technological solutions to problems, it is frequently still very difficult to translate these technical solutions into societal solutions. If you think about it very long you will undoubtedly conclude that this is true in many areas of activity. Let me give you one example from outside the marine and coastal field. Most of you know that we are on the verge of eliminating smallpox in the world. In fact, smallpox outbreaks now have been contained to two countries and when the war in Ethiopia and Somalia is resolved, it can be anticipated that smallpox also will be eradicated in those coutries. What is interesting for our purposes is that we have known how to eliminate smallpox for a number of years. Indeed, the smallpox vaccine was discovered in 1796 and President Thomas Jefferson even took an interest in its use. Yet it has taken us almost 200 years to come close to eradicating smallpox. It was the mid-1960s when national governments finally decided to get serious about the elimination of smallpox from the world and agreed to a World Health Organization program with those goals. Even then, the program could not have succeeded without sound and timely impact evidence concerning the cases of smallpox and the countries reporting them.

It is the process of translating apparent solutions to problems into actual solutions to societal problems that interests me most, perhaps because there are no easy ways of performing this task. The process is enoromously complex and it is difficult to facilitate the transferring of technical knowledge into societal programs which

180

actually work. It is of greatest importance to ask whether the societal programs are successful, and it cannot be assumed that programs are meeting their objectives simply because they are based on sound scientific principles. We need to use the evaluation research approach to determine whether the program that is implemented is achieving the desired objectives. In short, we need to take a hard-nosed look at whether the program is having an actual impact.

The evaluation research approach is potentially relevant for the examination of a wide range of marine and coastal issues. For example, it could be used to evaluate the impact of the California Coastal Act of 1976 or the extension of certain federal jurisdictions to include 200 miles of coastal waters. It could be helpful in the study of the impact of policy changes, projects, programs, program strategies, laws, court decisions, changes in institutional arrangements, funding levels, and other activities when it is difficult to sort out facts. Because of complexity and cost, the evaluation research approach should not be used to examine questions when the answer is already well known, and accepted without controversy, or to examine trivial questions.

There appear to be three different types of individuals who could benefit from the use of the evaluation research approach to study marine and coastal zone activities. Scholars could use the evaluation research approach to "add to knowledge available about social and interpersonal behavior and the social environment, and to explicate and refine the practice principles that underlie programming efforts." Policy-makers could use the evaluation research approach to generate knowledge on policy, program, and project effectiveness that can be used as feedback information to assist in the making of decisions regarding possible social action programs. The evaluation research approach also can be used to supply information needed for holding policy-makers accountable for their organization's actions. This latter use would be of greatest interest to those such as taxpayers and legislators to whom policy-makers are responsible.

Problems With Evaluation Research Approach

It can be anticipated that there will be a number of problems in using the evaluation research approach in the marine and coastal field. I will not list all of these problems, but I will note that they fall into two categories: (1) applied research problems; and, (2) research utilization problems.

The most serious difficulties in utilizing the evaluation research approach will be of an applied nature, although the seriousness of these problems will vary from study to study. We will have the usual measurement and data collection problems, and we may need to establish social indicator systems. The evaluation research approach is expensive, and that can present a problem. The level of methodological expertise needed to handle many research problems is high and it may be difficult to find qualified researchers, at least in the near future. Finally, it may be difficult, if not impossible, to identify the program goals and their relative importance. Those who doubt this last point should simply consult the California Coastal Act of 1976 for an education.

After execution of a study there will still be serious limitations in the use of the evaluation research results by policy-makers. In our governmental system the decisions are made through a process where political considerations are very important. Even if we produce sophisticated scientific impact studies, they will be only part of the relevant information considered by the elected officials and bureaucrats who make the decisions. The best that we can hope to do is to see to it that there are meaningful evaluation research studies which might assist policy-makers in undertaking decisions. The major research utilization problems will revolve around the fact that marine and coastal policies and programs are the result of political processes which tend to emphasize factors other than effectiveness evidence regarding ongoing activities and the fact that the timing of relatively fixed policy-making processes means that the use of the evaluation research approach to provide timely feedback will be greatly constrained.

We do not yet have a good understanding of the applied research and research utilization problems in the marine and coastal field, although we are working on them. It is possible, however, to offer a tentative judgment on the utility of the evaluation research approach in the marine and coastal field, one that is based on the work that we have done so far. It appears that the potential utility of the evaluation research approach is limited in terms of the percentage of activities that can be studied, but that a significant contribution could be made in those situations when it is possible to employ the approach.

Why should consideration be given to using the evaluation research approach in the marine and coastal field? The answer is: because we do not know which policies and programs will work, because we need information on the actual impact of policies and programs in order to improve them, and because the evaluation research approach holds forth the promise of providing this information for us.

Carol H. Weiss has noted that: "The (evaluation) research process takes more time and costs more money than offhand evaluations that rely on intuition, opinion, or trained sensibility, but it provides a rigor that is particularly important when (1) the outcomes to be evaluated are complex, hard to observe, made up of many elements reacting in diverse ways; (2) the decisions that will follow are important and expensive; and (3) evidence is needed to convince other people about the validity of the conclusions."[10] These conditions frequently confront policy-makers in the marine and coastal field. They should use the evaluation research approach when this happens. The evaluation research approach could be especially helpful to policy-makers in demonstrating their organization's accomplishments to those to whom they are responsible, especially those who are paying for the activities. Scholars also should use the evaluation research methodology when it is appropriate to do so.

Some of us at the Insitute for Marine and Coastal Studies at the University of Southern California hope to make a contribution by clarifying the applied research and the research utilization problems of the evaluation research approach in the marine and coastal field. We hope to learn more about which impact hypotheses are correct and to learn more about when to use the evaluation research approach to study marine and coastal policies and programs. At this point it seems clear that the difficulties in the application of the evaluation research approach are not sufficient to preclude its utility in the marine and coastal context. If properly used, the evaluation research methodology has the potential for providing reliable evidence for use in the marine and coastal field.

Alice M. Rivlin has argued: "Until programs are organized so that analysts can learn from them and systematic experimentation is undertaken on a significant scale, prospects seem dim for learning how to produce better social services."[11] It is frequently the case that there is no solid basis for knowing what impact marine and coastal policies and programs have had, and this is true of local, state, and national activities. I believe that we need to understand better the impacts of marine and coastal programs, whatever they are. I believe that we need to place special emphasis on asking and answering hard-nosed questions on the impact of marine and coastal policies and programs. The best way to improve the quality of research on these questions in the marine and coastal field is to improve the way in which questions are asked and answers are obtained. Clearly the ideas of the evaluation research approach can be of help in this undertaking.

Notes

1. For a listing of the experimental studies see Robert F. Boruch, "Bibliography: Illustrative Randomized Field Experiments for Planning and Evaluation," (Evanston, Illinois, Northwestern University, 1974), mimeo.

2. Cf. *Evaluation Studies Review Annual* (Beverly Hills, California: Sage Publications, annually starting in 1976).

3. Elmer L. Struening and Marcia Guttentag, eds., *Handbook of Evaluation Research,* Volume 1 (Beverly Hills, California: Sage Publications, 1975) and Marcia Guttentag and Elmer L Struening, eds., *Handbook* of *Evaluation Research,* Volume 2 (Beverly Hills, California: Sage Publications, 1975).

4. Cf. *Effectiveness Auditing in Government Administration, Goals and Methods for Examining the Effectiveness of Central Government in Sweden, Summary of a Report of the Swedish National Audit Bureau 1970,* The Swedish National Audit Bureau.

5. Joseph S. Wholey, John W. Scanlon, Hugh G. Duffy, James S. Fukumoto, and Leona M. Vogt, *Federal Evaluation Policy: Analyzing The Effects of Public Programs* (Washington, D.C.: The Urban Institute, 1973): p. 19.

6. The basic works are Donald T. Campbell and Julian C. Stanley, *Experimental and Quasi-Experimental Designs for Research* (Chicago: Rand McNally, 1963); Donald T. Campbell, "Reforms as Experiments," *American Psychologist* 24 (1969): 409-29; Donald T. Campbell and H. Laurence Ross, "The Connecticut Crackdown on Speeding: Time Series Data in Quasi-Experimental Analysis," *Law and Society Review* 3 (1968): pp. 33-53; H. Laurence Ross, Donald T. Campbell, and Gene V. Glass, "Determining the Social Effects of a Legal Reform: The British 'Breathalyser' Crackdown of 1967," *American Behavioral Scientist* 13 (1970): pp. 439-509; Henry Riecken, Robert F. Boruch,

Donal T. Campbell, Nathan Caplan, Thomas K. Glennan, Jr., John W. Pratt, Albert Rees, and Walter Williams, *Social Experimentation: A Method for Planning Social Intervention* (New York: Academic Press, 1974); Donald T. Campbell, "Assessing the Impact of Planned Social Change," in Gene M. Lyons, Ed., *Social Research and Public Policies: The Dartmouth/OECD Conference* (Hanover, New Hampshire: University Press of New England, 1975): pp. 3-45; Thomas D. Cook and Donald T. Campbell, "The Design and Conduct of Quasi-Experiments and True Experiments in Field Settings," in M. D. Dunnette, ed., *Handbook of Industrial and Organizational Research* (Chicago: Rand McNally, 1976): pp. 223-326; and, Donald T. Campbell and Robert F. Boruch, "Making the Case for Randomized Assignment to Treatments by Considering the Alternatives: Six Ways in Which Quasi-Experimental Evaluations in Compensatory Education Tend to Underestimate Effects," in Carl A. Bennett and Arthur A. Lumsdaine, eds., *Evaluation and Experiment: Some Critical Issues in Assessing Social Program* (New York: Academic Press, 1975): pp. 195-296.

7. Cf. Francis W. Hoole, *Evaluation Research and Development Activities* (Beverly Hills, California: Sage Publications, forthcoming 1978).

8. For an analysis of the smallpox eradication program of the World Health Organization see Francis W. Hoole, "Evaluating the Impact of International Organizations," *International Organization* 31 (1977): pp. 541-63.

9. Ilene N. Bernstein and Howard E. Freeman, *Academic and Entrepreneurial Research: The Consequences of Diversity in Federal Evaluation Studies* (New York: Russell Sage Foundation, 1975): pp. 1.

10. Carol H. Weiss, *Evaluation Research: Methods of Assessing Program Effectiveness* (Englewood Cliffs, New Jersey: Prentice-Hall, 1972): pp. 2.

11. Alice M. Rivlin, *Systematic Thinking for Social Action* (Washington, D.C.: The Brooking Institution, 1971): p. 64.

Part IV
Getting Our Own House in Order

13

Sea Power and National Ocean Policy —
Fantasies and Facts

Don Walsh

How can our nation use the sea? Uses of the sea require "sea power" which I define as an instrument of national policy. Unfortunately I contend that we suffer in the United States from "sea power sickness." What we might do to recover from our malaise is the subject of this chapter.

The national ability to use the sea involves a four-step process. The first step is simply acquisition of scientific knowledge of the sea. The principal product of oceanography, the scientific study of the sea, is one thing: <u>predictive information</u>. This is information about the marine environment that can be applied to man's uses of the sea. For example, this predictive information could concern the location and quality of fish stocks; which could lead to obvious payoffs in fish catches; or knowledge of subsea floor geological structures which may lead to gas and oil resources; or better advanced warning of marine weather so that we might increase the safe operation of ships.

The second process level is ocean engineering --the application of engineering principles to uses of the sea, to build machines and equipment to do work in the sea. But the fact of being able to build something does not itself indicate it is useful.

The third level is economics and public policy. This is where we determine if the work is useful. The economic test, of course, is rather obvious. Can you do something in or on the sea to produce a profit? This is the basis for establishing any business enterprise.

On the other hand, the "public policy" test is less precise. Perhaps the Navy is the best

example. Government defines operating a Navy as
an important use of the sea. It fails the economic
test, but there is no question that it is vital
for our national security. Another more pacific
example: in some developing parts of the world, a
government may set up a national fishing industry
because there is insufficient private capital for
this. Ultimately it will sell the industry to the
people who operate it as the industry becomes self-
sustaining. Public policy also helps determine
whether or not work at sea is useful.

The fourth and final level of process is also
a difficult set of problems. I call these "man-
made constraints on uses of the sea." Here we get
into the questions of national policies, law of
the sea, political processes, conservation of the
environment, cultural and ethnic problems. These
are issues that are very difficult to resolve.

By way of background, let us go back to 1889,
when Captain Alfred Mahan of the United States Navy
wrote the definitive work The Influence of Sea
Power on History, 1660-1873. He used the term "sea
power" to mean the study of uses of the sea, a sea
policy, a historical point of view, and national
destiny. Mahan talked about sea power in the sense
of this quality being a nation's total use of ocean
space--not only the military naval forces but also
the mercantile navy, the fishing navy, projection
of trade, commerce, conquest and exploration. His
views were popular, not only in the United States
but in Europe and Asia as well. The first foreign
book that was translated and extensively used in
Japan was Mahan's The Influence of Sea Power--which
the Emperor had translated for the benefit of the
Japanese Navy. The Japanese were coming out of a
400-year self-imposed isolation and Emperor Meiji
wanted his nation to have the most modern navy possible. Kaiser Wilhelm of Germany bought a great
supply of Mahan's book and issued one to every officer in his navy. It had great impact on naval
thinking of that time.

Since World War II the term "sea power" has
not enjoyed such a broad definition. Its usage
has been reduced to only the military element--
warships, submarines, aircraft carriers, etc.; I
prefer, however, to go back to the original definition. The essays in this book are, in fact,
about sea power. How do we use the sea? What are
the contemporary issues in science, technology,
economic questions, and man-made constraints on
uses of the sea?

Ocean policy hardly exists anywhere as a deliberate, stated policy of a state. But in the theoretical sense it is analogous to foreign policy. That is, how a nation relates its interests in a part of the world to interests of for shipping and communication, and an area for naval operations to enhance national security. The rule governing the ownership of the oceans for these activities was simplicity itself: there was open access for any purpose in all areas except for an narrow band of "territorial seas" adjacent to coastlines. Ships generally could sail where their captains pleased and they could establish private property rights in the fish or other resources that they found merely by capturing and hauling them onboard. The number of ocean demands and users was so small relative to the seemingly endless supply of space and resources that it made no sense economically to divide the oceans generally or to restrict access other nation states, is quite similar to how a nation relates its interests to others in the uses of the sea. When we talk about ocean policy, we are really taking about how we coherently plan and govern all of our national activities that relate to uses of the sea as an instrument of our national policy.

History of U.S. Ocean Policy

The United States has had a sort of de facto ocean policy at various times during its history. Unfortunately these times have related to periods of warfare, when things got organized very quickly and rather effectively with respect to uses of the sea. But ocean policy really has not been a consistent part of United States diplomacy or our national planning process during the last 200 years.

The founding fathers, in drafting the Constitution, provided that Congress should only "raise and support armies" and that no appropriations for that purpose should extend for more than two years. But when they talked about a navy, they said the United States shall, "provide and maintain a navy, "in other words, the appropriation for naval forces should be continuing. I suspect this came from memories, however distant, of Cromwell's England, when nobody trusted the army. They trusted the navy because it floated around the sea

190

and could not march on London. The navy was meant to be a permanent institution.

The schemes to manage our Navy in its early years varied widely. At one time the United States Navy had an Admiralty Board. They even talked about creating a "Ministry of Marine." The new republic looked at various approaches to governing our activities at sea and our uses of the sea. The early Congresses and Presidential administrations had an understanding of the fact that the fighting navy was only part of the enterprise. The Navy's station ships in the far-flung foreign ports were there to guard and to promote United States commercial interests. Therefore it was important to help stimulate development of our seagoing mercantile fleet, whaling, and fisheries.

And the United States did very well. In the 1840s a majority of the trade in the Pacific Ocean was carried in American flag ships. This was the era of the clipper ship, and American clipper ships were sailing rings around the elderly, dumpy British merchant ships. But the British did a very clever thing: they largely skipped the clipper ship stage and went directly to steam. British ships could then sail on any point of the wind with their auxiliary steam engines.

In the Civil War almost every type of modern weapon and tactic of naval warfare was applied. There were blockades of southern ports. There was estuarine warfare in the rivers of the West, similar to operations in Viet Nam. There was even an aircraft operation: Professor Lowe had a river barge from which he could launch a tethered balloon. In the balloon he placed an observer to report on troop movements behind southern lines (the first aircraft carrier?). They had submarines. The first combat of submarine and surface ship was the Confederate submersible, or submarine, Hunley versus a Federal Navy blockade ship outside Charleston Harbor. It was a one-way trip for the Hunley; the submarine sank the Federal surface ship but itself was trapped below its victim.

The Civil War also marked the end of the successful American merchant fleet. Once more the British did something clever. The Confederates had commerce raiding ships which roamed the seas of the world sinking Northern merchant vessels wherever they could find them. Most of the Union merchant ships were insured through European insurance companies. The Confederates, aided by British shipping interests, were able to convince these

191

insurance companies that they were going to sustain heavy losses because these Union merchant vessels were going to be sunk by raiders. The insurance companies either refused to insure or raised the costs so high that the Union merchant skippers could not afford them. That was very good for the British Merchant Marine, which had now driven the Yankee flag off the seas both with steam and a scare. A great majority of the American merchant fleet shifted to foreign flags (shifting to "flags of convenience" is nothing new). After the Civil War, the Congress unwisely did not permit these vessels to come back under the United States flag, and the United States Merchant Marine remained moribund until World War I.

In the Spanish-American War era, the superiority of United States ship design was again demonstrated by a Navy fleet arriving in Philippines after a long ocean voyage at top speed in a condition ready to go to war. The Navy's superior gunnery against the elderly Spanish fleet both there and in Cuba gave convincing example of the American Navy's readiness and material conditon.

The Navy's Atlantic Battle Fleet, called the "Great White Fleet," circumnavigated the globe in 1907-09 without any significant material or mechanical problem. This was the era of President Teddy Roosevelt showing the flag, the time of Mahan and of "Manifest Destiny." It was the appropriate time for an American to develop an inclusive theory of "sea power."

For the United States, World War I primarily was a war of transport rather than military operations involving combat at sea. Our principal role was convoying material goods and troops to Europe. We put together a very effective transport fleet together with the naval forces to protect them from submarines. For the first time American shipbuilding developed the techniques to build large numbers of steel ships in modern shipyards. Marine technologies were advanced significantly.

In World War II, naval operations were enormously successful once United States production capacity was activated. A demonstation of the ingenuity and success of "Yankee shipbuilding," is the case of Henry J. Kaiser. This successful industrialist was asked by President Roosevelt if he could turn his efforts to shipbuilding. He replied that he would--it was just a matter of organizing the men and material and doing it. But he did not want to depend too heavily upon the traditional naval architects, shipbuilders, shipwrights, and carpenters. He wanted, instead, people from the auto industry and locomotive factories. He stunned the traditional shipbuilding industry, which considered the ship to be a custom-made work of art. At the height of World War II, the Kaiser shipyard at Richmond, California, turned out an 8,000-ton Liberty ship from empty buildingway to launching in four days and eleven hours.

Americans do know how to gear up for effective ocean activity, but unfortunately these skills seem to manifest themselves only in wartime. Between wars, we have had such things as the 1921-22 Washington Conference for the Limitation of Naval Armaments where the politicians and diplomats "sunk more ships with the stroke of a pen than all the wars in the nation's history," as one disgruntled admiral said at the time. We have the technological and managerial know-how to be "Yankee mariners" again. But the skills are presently a bit rusty.

The United States came out of World War II as the largest and the most well-established sea power the world has ever known. We had the largest navy, the largest fishing fleet, the largest merchant fleet, and all the requisite technology and ability to work in the oceans. Now, thirty years later, we are fast becoming a second-rate sea power.

Present Ocean Policy

At present the United States Navy has about 460 ships. This is the smallest number of Naval vessels that we have had since 1939. While our newest warships are admittedly very capable units, they can still be in only one place at a time. As recently as 1968, we had over 1,000 vesels in the Navy. When one hears talk about the marvelous quality of our present vessels, as if this were an answer to the lesser numbers, I remember what the late airpower proponent, Alexander de Seversky, once said: "quantity is a quality in itself."

President Carter's recent action in cutting the Navy's proposed shipbuilding program by almost one-half does not encourage one to hope for a navy that has no peer in the world. We are now on the road to having a navy that is second best. This is not a comfortable prospect as we face the maritime challenge posed by the Soviet Union. Our national defense effort must have credibility at sea as well as in the air and on land.

The status of our merchant marine is also a cause for serious concern. Most analysts of maritime affairs believe that a sea power state should carry about 40-50 percent of its own trade in its national flag vessels. The United States Merchant Marine carries only about 6 percent of United States goods, on a tonnage basis. Our merchant fleet ranks about nineth in the world behind the United Kingdom, Russia, Japan, Greece, Norway, Liberia, France, and Panama. Since 98 percent of all world trade travels in ships at some point between the producer and the consumer, and since 88 percent of the dollar value of United States trade is carried by ships, it should be in the interest of the United States to build its merchant fleet to earn for itself more of the monies spent in the carriage of goods. With the majority of foreign merchant fleets being heavily subsidized by their governments, the money we pay for using these ships is in effect a transfer from the United States economy to foreign treasuries. The talk about reducing subsidies to our ships does not suggest a complete understanding of what it takes to be competitive in an industry where all the competition is openly subsidized.

This is not to say that we cannot manage our merchant marine assests more effectively. There is much that can be done to improve this area, but it is a gross oversimplification to blame the poor competitive position of United States shipping on the usual combination of high labor costs, high construction costs, and government subsidies. If we are to be a major maritime trading nation then we must have the seagoing assets to support the export and import of our trade. To leave this to foreign flag fleets invites others to control the economic lifelines of the United States.

The current Law of the Sea negotiations represent a far more serious problem with respect to future uses of the sea. Virtually the entire world community is involved in the largest international negotiation in the history of civilization working on developing an orderly legal framework for the 71 percent of our planet covered by water. Whether we get a law of the sea treaty or not, the political geography of ocean space will be changed permanently for all time. Involved will be issues of pollution, resource uses, transportation, marine sciences and freedom of navigation.

Closer to home, the lack of a timely deepwater port policy in this country has cost us dearly as a result of the energy crunch. The only place we can save anything on the import of petroleum is in the transport itself. We do not have a single port in the United States that can handle the most economically efficient large crude carriers (tankers displacing over 200,000 tons). Yet we are the world's major importer of hydrocarbons. We are beginning to take care of this problem. Because of our late start the solutions will be much more costly and difficult.

Cargo Preference

A final example would be the nonsense about cargo preference that we have just recently gone through. When the President's proposal to require shipment of a small fraction (about 9 percent) of United States oil imports in United States tankers was presented to Congress it was turned down. There was talk about what a "consumer ripoff" cargo preference would have been had it passed. It was said that foreign tankers could do the job cheaper. This is only a partial truth; it oversimplifies the problem. What actually happens is that we are going to continue to transfer the cost of carriage of our crude oil imports to foreign governments via their heavily subsidizied merchant fleets. A significant, though not the largest, part of our deficit in export/import balance goes to pay for carriage of petroleum. And we are paying this to foreign governments rather than to United States shippers. Nobody has looked at the numbers, they just say the price per barrel goes up because American ships are more expensive, but they do not consider the invisible marine carriage caused transfer to foreign governments.

All these indices of uses of the sea or sea power point in an unfavorable direction. This seems to indicate that the United States has not really concerned itself, in an institutional way, with how the government should be organized for effective uses of the sea.

There is a great gap today between "doing" and "regulation" in uses of the sea. What I mean by this is simply that in science and technology we can now do more things in and on the sea then we have the capability or sophistication for governing these activities. This gap is perhaps

195

fifteen to twenty years between the government process, and the ability of science and technology to
exploit the marine environment. Therefore, the
constraints on uses of the sea are not really in
the areas of scientific or technological knowledge. That is not to say we should not move ahead
on development in these areas, but rather if you
are thinking about a management matrix, the "critical path" is found in the political and policy
areas.

What is the basic flaw behind all this? It
begins with the fact that our national ocean programs are fractionalized and uncoordinated. We do
not have a national ocean policy. There are no
high-level advisors to counsel the chief executive
of the United States, the President. All of his
maritime advisors, the Secretary of the Navy, the
head of the Maritime Administration, the Admini-
strator of the National Oceanic and Atmospheric
Administration, Commandant of the Coast Guard, etc.
are sub-Cabinet level officers. They are one to
two levels removed from the cabinet, thus the
Cabinet officer for their particular agency is un-
derstandably concerned with many other things than
just maritime issues involving his department.
Therefore, the President does not have any direct
counsel among his many advisors on maritime issues
that is continuous and at a high level.

There is also a general lack of public interest and awareness in the stake we have in the
oceans. The Congressional committee structure to
consider ocean issues is fairly diffuse. A few
years ago there was an almost successful effort
within the House, through the Bolling Committee,
to cancel the House Merchant Marine and Fisheries
Committee in a reorganization move. While this
did not happen, it was one of the few committees
recommended for complete elinination.

"Fish don't vote!," one Congressmen has told
me. There are no voters in the oceans. That is a
cheap shot. Those that think this way will never
imagine nor advocate a "moon project" for the
oceans. As a result, we have no focal project in
the oceans. Space program funding versus ocean
program funding gives a useful index of the imbal-
ance. The Federal Ocean Program is budgeted between $1-2 billion a year, depending on how you
count. The national space program is funded at
more than $4 billion a year, two to four times
greater than the national ocean effort. This is
just the NASA budget. If you add in military

space programs the disproportion between space and ocean programs is much larger.

In the United States we keep adding new players in the ocean policy area. It is somewhat like counting baby spiders. The "statistical life in office" of a Presidential appointee in Washington is about twenty four months. This may incease with Mr. Carter's insistence that his appointees stay for four years. However, some of the national media are already predicting that some of the cabinet officers will be leaving before the end of this administration. In the oceans we are concerned with problems that perhaps will require decades to find the solutions. The necessary long-range policy formulations do not lend themselves to a tenty four month "life cycle" of appointed and elected policy makers.

In Congress the House turns over every two years. With the increase in more junior members, the average congressman is probably good for only about a year of productive work. The election is held in November and Congressmen take their seats in January. Then begins the organization at work of the new Congress. By the time they really get to work with hearings, legislation, etc., it is spring. A year later, next summer, they have to start running for office again. The public gets about one productive year out of Congressmen unless they are senior and/or have a very safe district. Then we may expect more productivity. With the Senators the situation is better. A six-year term allows them do do solid work before they have to worry about the ballot box.

We are dealing with different sets of short-term time constraints in the policy making process that impact upon a very long-term problem. The health of sea power in our country is not a short-term problem.

Federal Agencies Concerned with Oceans

How are we actually organized in the government today on ocean matters? There are about twenty-one different Federal agencies, department, and offices that have key concerns with the uses of the sea. As mentioned earlier, the Federal ocean budget, which is called the Federal Ocean Program, is about $1-2 billion a year. Most of these twenty-one agencies and offices approach the administration and Capitol Hill via different procedural paths. There is no real coordination or coherence in putting together their annual ocean activities presentations for budget allocation from the administration, or for their budgets being presented to the Congress. On the House side of Congress alone there are between thirteen and sixteen different committees that have partial responsibilities for ocean activities. This means there is an inherent lack of coherence in the House. On the Senate side there are about six different Senate committees that have ocean interests. There is no one ocean committee on either side. There used to be.

Before the National Security Act of 1947, which brought the Department of Defense into being and created the Air Force as a separate service, there were two Congressional defense committees: a Committee on Naval Affairs, and a Committee on War. The former was responsible for a wide range of sea power issues in addition to naval issues. Furthermore, the Secretary of the Navy and the Secretary of War were both Cabinet officers, so they directly advised the President of the United States.

When the Department of Defense was created as a result of the Act of 1947, there were three services each with a secretary under the overall direction of the Secretary of Defense. The Secretary of Defense became a Cabinet member but the Secretaries of War and Navy were dropped (the Air Force was never in the Cabinet). The Armed Forces Committee replaced the War and Naval Committees in both the House and Senate. Naval and sea power advice to the chief executive and to the Congress were moved one to two steps away from the primary "transmission belt" between the responsible official and the decision maker in the White House or on the Hill.

The result was that sea power issues got pushed slightly to one side. The United States has had to deal with many recent serious problems that are ocean-oriented without a coherent ocean policy or a framework for formulating one. Some examples: the 1973 oil crisis; the Nixon Doctrine of getting out of overseas bases, the U.N. Law of the Sea negotiations of the last twelve years, and the lack of a deepwater port system.

The United States' rather poor performance in the long Law of the Sea negotiations since 1958 is a direct result of the lack of an adequate ocean policy-making framework. The departments of State,

Defense, Interior, Treasury, and Commerce have jockeyed for position and pushed their particular interest, with different interests dominant at different times, and presidential administrations have changed--all at the expense of a coherent, consistent negotiating stance.

As mentioned earlier, our energy shortage could have been greatly mitigated if we had dveloped superports that could accept the world's more than 400 supertankers which can deliver oil at greatly reduced shipping costs. But such port facilities take ten to fifteen years to plan and develop. This requires an overall national plan embodying authority and responsibility; allocation of resources, and finally, someone who is ultimately in charge.

Important, long-term issues--including a national ocean policy or "sea power"--have to be institutionalized. Policy is the product of a mechanism or framework. The United States must have such a framework. There are various proposals for the form such a national ocean policy making organization would take. I do not espouse any particular one, nor do I advocate something like a "wet NASA." But the ultimate choice has to be a thoroughly workable mechanism as opposed to a textbook perfect plan.

Need for Ocean Policy Mechanism

What is the cure for our national sea power sickness? We need a national ocean policy mechanism that insures coordination of all marine activities of our nation. I am not suggesting a super agency. There is a difference between a rational solution and the idea of a "wet NASA" sweeping everything together into one agency. I do support reorganization in the executive branch of the government along functional lines. We have a "department of food" (Agriculture), a "department of money" (Treasury), etc. I see nothing wrong with these various departments continuing to have ocean maritime functions within them. Just because it is wet, is insufficient argument for transfer to a special "wet agency."

Right now many of these departments are engaged in unwarranted competition, trying to grab maritime missions away from their neighbors. Fighting with each other is wasteful, with the taxpayer getting poor value for his money. But this infighting occurs because no one is in charge at the supra-cabinet level. I believe we ought to go back to fundamentals. We need better organization along functional lines in the executive branch.

In addition, there needs to be a better Congressional "pathway" in the ocean area. I steered away from the term "reorganization" here because it is a near-impossible task. But Congressional handling of ocean issues is indeed very complex and perhaps more confusing than the way they are presently handled in the executive branch.

Up to this point I have discussed the domestic lack of continuity. But this is also reflected in the international scene. There are about 160 nation states in the world today. Of the 160, about 130 are coastal states, and of these coastal states, 86 percent are developing nations. Thus, the vast majority of coastal states are third-world nations. These nations are, in fact, sea powers--any nation that has a coastline quaifies. Sea power can be active or passive as there is potential in many of these places to develop effective uses of the sea. In the United Nations Law of the Sea Conference they are outvoting the developed, seagoing nations. They are exercising their own interests. They represent sea power on a different level, but nevertheless they are exercising international influence based on maritime issues. There is faulty understanding in many cases, but political force is being exercised with respect to ocean issues. When the first round of Law of the Sea Conferences was held in 1958 and 1960, there were about ninety nations in the world. But when the second round began in late 1973 the number had increased to 156 nations. The majority, which are developing coastal nations, have very different goals from the developed nations. A tremendous strain has been built into the international political process. This is a good example of the problem of accommodating the political process to the technical, scientific, and economic knowledge we have about how to use the sea. It is a very difficult and complex question.

On the hopeful side, about three years ago the Senate initiated a National Ocean Policy Study. Under the direction of Senators Magnuson and Hollings, the Senate has been holding hearings and writing reports on various aspects of marine issues facing our country. By and large most of the work has been good, and we may see some beneficial product although as yet no significant legislation has resulted.

In 1975 the House of Representatives started an informal ocean policy group under the subcommittee on Oceanography (of the House Committee on Merchant Marine and Fisheries). In 1977 President Carter asked his Presidential Reogranization Plan staff to make a study of ocean policy questions, and how the administration should be organized to discharge these responsibilities. That study was delivered to the President in 1978. What changes will be made as a result of this work is not clear at this time.

All of these activities may help, but leadership must come from the chief executive. The Congress cannot take the role of leadership in defining our national ocean policies.

Among the maritime powers the Soviet Union, which historically has not been a "traditional" sea power, seems to understand these matters very well. Their development as a great sea power in only sixteen years has been the result of both commitment and continuity. For example, Admiral Gorshkov, who is both their chief of naval operations and secretary of the navy combined, has been in this job nearly two decades. This is continuity. Not simply continuity of people, but continuity of _policy_ and _institutions_. They have learned how to harmonize their seapower. Their fishing fleet, research fleet, mercantile fleet and their naval forces work all over the world in coordinated activities which are programmed by central authority. It is interesting that a nation not traditionally a sea power has within a space of a decade and a half learned the rules of the game: how to move complex fleets, scientifc, fishing fleets, and naval fleets all over the globe to help extend their interest and their influence throughout the world.

In the United States we need to build the public awareness of the problem. We need to develop a historic pride in the "Yankee mariner" and an interest in returning him to the oceans of the world. This will require a committed involvement by the membership of the maritime community. We have to get involved in political process, we just can not leave it to a few people--it will never it get done.

Can the Yankee mariner make a comeback? I think so. We have the skills; we know how to mobilize capital, technology, management and man-

power. We have done it in the past. We have been
a great sea power. But we need the interest of
the people and of their government. We need the
policy to be allocated by the government as well
as allocation of resources. And our leaders must
lead.

The promised reorganization of ocean programs
in the government under Mr. Carter's Presidential
Reogranization Plan may be implemented. However,
it is also they way of Washington that it may be
deferred even further as time goes by, as other
"higher priority" concerns keep stepping in front
of it. It is a long-term problem and it requires
a long-term commitment on the part of leadership.
Unfortunately much of our government process lives
in a short-term world. Until we can isolate that
long-term problem and really work on it, I am not
too optimistic.

Suggestions for Further Reading

OCEAN SCIENCE AND TECHNOLOGY

Ambouchine, W. A., and Sternberg, R. W. *The World Ocean, An Introduction to Oceanography.* Englewood, New Jersey: Prentice-Hall, 1973.

Doumani, G. A., *Ocean Wealth and Policy.* Rochelle Park, New Jersey: Hayden Book Company, 1973.

Gross, M. Grant. *Oceanography* (3rd edition). Columbus, Ohio: Charles E. Merrill Publishing Company, 1976.

Goodfellow, R. *Underwater Engineering.* Tulsa, Oklahoma: Petroleum Publishing Company, 1977.

Gullion, E. A., *Uses of the Sea.* Englewood, New Jersey: Prentice-Hall, 1968.

Mining in the Outer Continental Shelf and in the Deep Ocean. National Academy of Sciences, 1975.

Vetter, R. C., ed., "Oceanography, The Last Frontier." *Voice of America Series,* United States Information Agency, 1974.

Offshore Technology Conference (1970-1979). *Proceedings,* Annual Meeting, Houston, Texas.

"The Ocean: Special Issue" *Scientific American* 221:3 (September 1969), pp. 1-228.

"Renewable Ocean Energy Sources." *Part I, Ocean Thermal Energy Conversion.* Office of Technology Assessment, Congress of the United States, 1978.

OCEAN POLICY

Brown, Seyom, Cornell, Nina, W., Fabian, Larry A., and Brown Weiss, Edith Brown. *Regimes for the Ocean, Outer Space, and Weather.* Washington: Brookings, 1977.

Christy, Francis T., Jr. and Scott, Anthony. *The Common Wealth in Ocean Fisheries.* Baltimore: Johns Hopkins University Press, 1965.

Committee on Commerce. U.S. Senate. *Soviet Oceans* Development 94th Congress, 2d Session.

Friedheim, Robert L., "Understanding The Debate On Ocean Resources." *Monograph Series In World Affairs,* Vol. 6: Monograph No. 3: University of Denver, 1968-69.

Grotius, Hugo. *The Freedom of the Seas*, edited by James Scott Brown. New York: Oxford University Press, 1916.

Hardin, Garrett and Baden, John, eds. *Managing The Commons.* San Francisco: Freeman, 1977.

Hollick, Ann L., and Osgood, Robert E. *New Era of Ocean Politics.* Baltimore: Johns Hopkins University Press, 1974.

Luttwak, Edward N. *The Political Uses of Sea Power.* Baltimore: Johns Hopkins University Press, 1974.

McDougal, Myres and Burke, William. *The Public Order of the Oceans*. New Haven: Yale University Press, 1962.

Office of Technology Assessment. Congress of the United States. *Establishing a 200 Mile Fisheries Zone.* Washington: Government Printing Office, 1977.

OCEAN GEOLOGY

Emery, K. O. *The Sea Off Southern California — A Modern Habitat of Petroleum.* New York: John Wiley, 1960.

Howell, David G. (ed.), *Aspects of the Geologic History of the California Continental Borderland.* Amer. Association Petroleum Geologists Miscellaneous Pub. 24, 1976.

Shepard, F. P., and Emery, K. O., *Submarine Topography Off the California Coast — Canyons and Tectonic Interpretations.* Geologic Society American, Spec. Paper 31.

Wertenbaker, William, *The Floor of the Sea: Maurice Ewing and the Search to Understand the Earth*. Boston: Little, Brown, 1974.

ENERGY FROM THE OCEANS

Energy Fact Book. Oceanography Sources Chapter XX. ONR Arlington, Virginia, February, 1977.

Energy From the Oceans: Fact or Fantasy. Proceedings, Jan. 27-28. Raleigh, North Carolina, Report No. 76-1, UNC-SG, 76-04, 1976.

Glalwel, J. S., and Warnick, C. C. "Small Hydro — A Second Chance." *Water International* 4 (No. 1) March, 1979.

Gray, T. J. and Gashus, O. K. *Tidal Power*. New York: Plenum Press, 1972.

Kash, Don E. et al. *Energy Under the Oceans: A Technology Assessment of Outer Continental Shelf Oil and Gas Operations.* Norman: University of Oklahoma Press, 1973.

Kaufman, D. Z., "Water For Project Independence." *Water Spectrum.* U.S. Army Corps of Engineers, Vol. 6, No. 4. Winter 1974-75.

Ocean Thermal Energy Conversion (OTEC) Program. DOE/ET-002/1-UC-64, Program Summaries.

Thirring, Hans. *Energy For Man: From Windmills To Nuclear Power.* New York: Harper & Row, 1958.

Wave and Salinity Gradient Energy Conversion, Workshop Proceedings, May 24-26, Newark, Delaware. ERDA Report, No. C00-2956-1. Conf. 760564, 1976.

Wayne, W. W. Jr., *Tidal Power Study for the U.S.* ERDA March. DGE/2293-3, Vol. 2. Distribution Category, UC-13, 1977.

SPACE OCEANOGRAPHY

Badgely, P. Miloy, L., and Childs, L., eds. *The Oceans from Space,* Houston, Texas: Gulf Publishing Company, 1969.

Davis, M., and Murray, B. *The View from Space*, New York: Columbia University Press, 1971.

Ewing, G., ed. *Oceanography from Space*, Woods Hole Oceanographic Institute, Reference No. 65-10, 1965.

Lintz, J., and Simmonett, D. *Remote Sensing of the Environment*. Reading, Mass: Addison-Wesley, 1976.

U.S. Government Printing Office, *Mission to Earth: Landsat Views the World*, NASA SP-360, Washington, D.C., Stock No. 033-000-00659-4, 1976.

Williams, R., and Carter, W., eds. *ERTS-1: A Window on Our Planet*, Geological Survey Professional Paper 929, U.S. Government Printing Office, Washington, D.C., Stock No. 024-001-02757-7.

OCEAN ECONOMICS

Eckert, Ross D., *The Enclosure of Ocean Resources: Economics and the Law of the Sea*. Stanford: Hoover Institution Press, 1979.

"Exploitation of Deep Ocean Minerals: Regulatory Mechanisms and United States Policy." *Journal of Law and Economics* 17 (1974): 117-42.

Clarkson, Kenneth W., "International Law, U.S. Seabeds Policy and Ocean Resource Development." *Journal of Law and Economics* 17 (1974): 117-42.

Amacher, Ryan and Sweeney, Richard James, eds. *The Law of the Sea: U.S. Interests and Alternatives*. Washington, D.C.: American Enterprise Institute for Public Policy Research, 1976.

Demsetz, Harold. "Toward a Theory of Property Rights." *American Economic Review, Papers and Proceedings* 57 (May 1967): 347-59.

Coase, R. H. "United States Policy Regarding the Law of the Seas." In *Mineral Resources of the Deep Seabed*, U.S. Congress, Senate, committee on Interior and Insular Affairs, Hearings before the Subcommittee on Minerals, Materials and Fuels, 93d Cong., 2d Session., pt. 2, March 5, 6, 11, 1974, pp. 1160-1174.

Friedman, Alan E. "The Economics of the Common Pool: Property Rights in Exhaustible Resources." *U.C.L.A. Law Review* 18 (1971): 855-87.

Gordon H. Scott. "The Economic Theory of a Common-Property Resource: The Fishery." *Journal of Political Economy* 62 (1954): 124-42.

Cummins, Philip A., Logue, Dennis E., Tollison, Robert D., and Willett, Thomas D. "Oil Tanker Pollution Control: Design Criteria vs. Effective Liability Assessment." *Journal of Maritime Law and Commerce* 7 (1975): 169-206.

OCEAN ENVIRONMENT

Goldberg, Edward D., *A Guide to Marine Pollution*. New York: Gordon and Breach Science Publications, 1972.

Hood, Donald W., ed. *Impingement of Man on the Oceans*. New York: Wiley-Interscience, 1971.

Johnston, R. ed., *Marine Pollution*, London: Academic Press, 1976.

National Research Council Study Panel. *Assessing Potential Ocean Pollutants*, National Academy of Sciences, Washington, D.C. 1975.

Ophuls, William. *Ecology and the Politics of Scarcity.* San Francisco: Freeman, 1977.

Pearson, Charles. *International Marine Environment Policy: The Economic Dimension.* Baltimore: Johns Hopkins University Press, 1975.

Shinn, Robert A. *The International Politics of Pollution.* New York: Praeger Publications, 1974.

Sibthorp, M. M. *Ocean Pollution: A Survey and Some Suggestions for Control.* London: The David Davies Memorial Institute of International Studies, 1969.

U.S. Office of Technology Assessment. *Oil Transportation by Tankers: An Analysis of Marine Pollution and Safety Measures,* U.S. Congress, Washington, D.C., 1975.

National Oceanic and Atmospheric Administration, *Report to the Congress on Ocean Pollution, Overfishing, and Offshore Development*, U.S. Department of Commerce, Washington, D.C., 1972.

MARINE MAMMALS

Barbour, J. A. *In the Wake of the Whale*. New York: Macmillan Company, 1969.

Hardy, A. *Great Waters: A Voyage of Natural History to Study Whales, Plankton and the Waters of the Southern Ocean*. New York: Harper and Row, 1967.

Mackintosh, N. A. *The Stocks of Whales*. London: Fishing News Ltd., 1965.

Norris, K.S. *The Porpoise Watcher.* New York: W. W. Norton & Co., 1974.

Schevill, W. E., ed. *The Whale Problem: A Status Report.* Cambridge, Mass.: Harvard University Press, 1974.

LAW OF THE SEA NEGOTIATIONS

Anon. "Scramble for the Ocean's Treasure," *To the Point International* (January 1978), pp. 14-18.

Charney, Jonathan, "Law of the Sea: Breaking the Deadlock," *Foreign Affairs* 55:3 (April 1977), pp. 598-629.

Oxman, Bernard, "The Third United Nations Conference of the Law of the Sea: The Seventh Session (1978), *American Journal of International Law* (January 1979), pp. 1-41.

Miles, Edward, ed. "Special Issue: Restructuring Ocean Regimes: Implications of the Third United Nations Conference on the Law of the Sea." *International Organization* 31:2 (Spring, 1977), pp. 151-384.

Pardo, Arvid. *The Common Heritage of Mankind.* Valetta, Malta: University of Malta Press, 1975.

Pardo, Arvid. "The Evolving Law of the Sea," *Ocean Yearbook I.* Chicago: University of Chicago Press, 1978, pp. 9-37.

Raymond, Nicholas. "Sea Law: the Unpleasant Options," *Ocean World* (January 1978), pp. 4-12.

Richardson, Elliott. "An Impasse on Seabeds," *Sea Power* (September 1977), pp. 23-28.

MARINE TRANSPORTATION

Bragaw, Louis K., Marcus, Henry S., Raffaele, Gary C., and Townley, James R. *The Challenge of Deepwater Terminals*. Lexington, Mass: Lexington, 1975.

Committee on the Impact of Maritime Services on Local Populations, Maritime Transportation Research Board; Commission on Socio-technical Systems, National Research Council (National Academy of Sciences). *Public Involvement in Maritime Facility Development*. Washington: National Research Council, 1979.

Lawrence, Samuel A. *International Sea Transport: The Years Ahead*. Lexington, Mass: Lexington, 1972.

Lawrence, Samuel A. *United States Merchant Shipping: Policies and Politics*. Washington: Brookings, 1966.

Marcus, Henry S. *Federal Port Policy in the United States*. Cambridge: MIT Press, 1976.

Marx, Daniel, Jr. *International Shipping Cartels*. Princeton: Princeton University Press, 1953.

M'Gonigle, R. Michael, and Zacker, Mark W. *Pollution, Politics and International Law*. Berkeley and Los Angeles: University of California Press, 1979.

Mostert, Noel. *Supership*. New York: Warner Books, 1975.

Nathan, Robert R. Associates, Inc. *A Study to Determine U.S. Port Needs, a Report for U.S. Army Corps of Engineers*. Washington: Nathan, 1972.

EVALUATION RESEARCH AND COASTAL ZONE MANAGEMENT

Devanney, J. W. II, Ashe, G., Parkhurst, B. *Parable Beach: A Primer In Coastal Zone Economics*, Cambridge: MIT Press, 1976.

Ducsik, Dennis W. *Shoreline For The Public: A Handbook of Social, Economic, and Legal Considerations Regarding Public Recreational Use of the Nation's Coastal Shoreline*. Cambridge: MIT Press, 1974.

Guttentag, Marcia, and Struening, Elmer L., eds. *Handbook of Evaluation Research*. Vol. 1. Beverly Hills, California: Sage Publications, 1975.

Hoole, Francis W. *Evaluation Research and Development Activities*. Beverly Hills, California: Sage Publications, 1978.

Ketchem, Bostwick H. *The Water's Edge: Critical Problems of the Coastal Zone*. Cambridge: MIT Press, 1972.

Patton, Michael Quinn. *Utilization Focused Evaluation*. Beverly Hills, California: Sage Publications, 1978.

Rossi, Peter H., Freeman, Howard E., and Wright, Sonia R. *Evaluation: A Systematic Approach*. Beverly Hills, California: Sage Publications, 1979.

Riechen, Henry, Bovich, Robert F., Campbell, Donald T., Caplan, Nathan, Glennan, Thomas K. Jr., Pratt, John W., Rees, Albert and Williams, Walter. *Social Experimentation: A Method for Planning Social Intervention.* New York: Academic Press, 1974.

Struening, Elmer L., and Guttentag, Marcia, eds. *Handbook of Evaluation Research.* Vol. 1. Beverly Hills, California: Sage Publications, 1975.

Weiss, Carol H. *Evaluation Research: Methods of Assessing Program Effectiveness.* Englewood Cliffs, New Jersey: Prentice-Hall, 1972.

NATIONAL OCEAN POLICY

Commission on Marine Science, Engineering and Resources. *Our Nation and the Sea: A Plan for National Action.* Washington: Government Printing Office, 1969.

Friedheim, Robert L. and Bowen, Robert and others. "Assessing the State of the Art in National Ocean Policy Studies," *Ocean Development and International Law Journal* (forthcoming, January 1980).

Gamble, Jr., John K. *Maritime Policy.* Lexington, Mass.: Lexington, 1977.

Mangone, Gerald J. *Marine Policy for America.* Lexington, Mass.: Lexington, 1977.

Walsh, Don. "Organization for Ocean Management: Centralization vs. Functionalization." In National Advisory Committee on Ocean and Atmosphere, *Reorganizing the Federal Effort in Oceanic and Atmospheric Affairs,* Vol. II. Washington: Government Printing Office, 1979.

Wenk, Edward Jr. *The Politics of the Ocean.* Seattle: University of Washington Press, 1972.

U.S. Department of Commerce. *U.S. Ocean Policy in the 1970s: Status and Issues.* Washington: Government Printing Office, 1978.